Colleges and the
Urban Poor

Colleges and the Urban Poor

The Role of Public Higher Education in Community Service

Doris B. Holleb
University of Chicago

Lexington Books
D.C. Heath and Company
Lexington, Massachusetts
Toronto   London

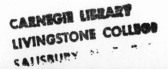

Table of Contents

List of Tables

Foreword

Everyone today requires some schooling, and a large fraction of the population needs more than high school education to carry on complex occupations and to furnish community leadership. The increasing demand for higher education, so dramatically seen in the rapid growth in college enrollments, is not merely a response to the rising aspirations of a society that sees affluence within its reach. It is also essential to the maintenance and development of our civilization.

The extraordinary developments of contemporary civilization are based on extensive applications of knowledge and education—the central concerns of colleges and universities. Our systems of producing, distributing and consuming goods, our methods of government, our civic and family activities, even our personal ways of seeking fuller meaning and satisfaction in our lives are complex and interdependent. They cannot be fully understood, utilized or appreciated without education that takes us beyond the limited environment of our own direct experience.

Yet in the current upsurge of college attendance and the growing percentage of Americans who are college graduates, those who are poor and those who come from minority groups are very inadequately represented. This is particularly obvious in the cities. The urban poor are not being served by our colleges in the ways and to the extent that those from homes with greater incomes, and those from majority groups, have been aided. This fact is now widely recognized, and many colleges are currently seeking to right the balance. But their efforts are often based on a simplistic view of the problems involved.

This book furnishes the first published comprehensive analysis of the complex conditions that must be dealt with in order to make substantial progress in providing higher educational opportunities for the poor and in serving more fully the educational needs of the inner city. The problems are not simple, and the factors involved are intertwined and often interacting. Nevertheless, the author has been able to unravel the tangled web and to analyze the complexities with such care and clarity that the significant aspects are identified and those features of greatest influence are brought into focus. A blend between the general and the concrete is achieved by using public higher education in Illinois to illustrate the analysis and to demonstrate the application of the approach and the feasibility of the kinds of solutions outlined.

The treatment is unique in presenting the problems as viewed by the students as well as by the colleges. This enables the reader to perceive the stark reality of the obstacles faced by the urban poor who seek higher education, as well as the outlook of the colleges who have failed to recognize the students' difficulties and have even created some of them. If the students from the inner cities are to be served, their aspirations, their problems and their resources must be understood. Furthermore, the capabilities and the limitations of the college must be assessed so that an effective program can be devised and developed that can actually be implemented. This principle is basic to the author's treatment. It makes the volume a guide to planning and action rather than another hortatory appeal.

The treatment is also unique in its realistic appraisal of the promise and problems of the community colleges and for its straightforward discussion of the educational problems of segregation, a subject often ignored in the literature of higher education. In addition, the direct relevance of scholarly research and teaching to community service and the need for deep-seated institutional changes are emphasized throughout.

The book is an example of the contributions that social scientists can make to those responsible for the development of public policy. The analysis presented and the kinds of solutions outlined are based upon detailed studies conducted by the author under the auspices of the Center for Urban Studies of the University of Chicago. The wide variety of data collected for the study of Illinois higher education is brought together and analyzed in ways that throw factual light on issues that are hotly controversial and often deliberated without benefit of comprehensive information. In this way it is a model of procedure for dealing with other thorny problems of public policy. The treatment is objective, thoughtful and balanced.

Because this book focuses on a critical problem with which colleges and universities must deal and because it treats the problem comprehensively, and the possible solutions imaginatively, it is recommended reading for all who are concerned with the future of higher education. It should not only be read in full but used as a continuing reference by those working out college programs for serving the urban poor.

Ralph W. Tyler
Director Emeritus, Center
for Advanced Studies in the
Behavioral Sciences, and
Acting Director, Social Science
Research Council

Preface

This book is an outgrowth of an earlier study undertaken in 1969 for the Illinois Board of Higher Education in connection with the preparation of a *Master Plan for Higher Education: Phase III*. Recognizing the need for a systematic assessment of problems in urban poverty areas and of the related capacities of state universities and colleges, the Board, in consultation with members of the Illinois Council on Community Services and Continuing Education, invited the Center for Urban Studies of the University of Chicago to explore the subject. In studying the role of higher education in community service, they suggested that research priorities be given to human development problems, and in the light of state planning needs, three functional fields were singled out for special attention, namely, health, recreation and social service.

The chief themes discussed in this second, more comprehensive study are all foreshadowed in the Illinois report, and the emphasis on human service fields remains. The writer is very grateful to the members and staff of the Illinois Board and Council for directing attention to this important subject.

The Illinois study was supported with funds appropriated under the federal Higher Education Act of 1965 (P.L. 89-329), as amended, fiscal year 1969. The act has two major objectives: (1) "the solution of community problems," and (2) "strengthening community service programs of colleges and universities." In presenting the legislation to the Congress in 1965, the Secretary of Health, Education and Welfare made the following remarks.

Today, 70 percent of our population live in urban areas. Much work lies ahead to fully examine the meaning to the Nation of this shift in homes, occupations, and social problems. While land grant colleges still provide the best schools of agriculture, few adequate programs exist that meet head-on the problems of urban life.

We believe higher education can help find the answers. The unique and invaluable resources of the Nation's great universities can deal with such contemporary problems as poverty and community development.[1]

Concurring with the spirit of the above statement, the writer, Research Associate at the Center for Urban Studies at the University of Chicago, agreed to direct the research which led, first, to a report for the state board and, ultimately, to this book. The financial support of the U.S. Department of Health, Education and Welfare in the initial, Illinois-centered phase of the work is gratefully acknowledged.

Many colleagues, faculty and students of the Center for Urban Studies, participated in early discussions and data-gathering for the Illinois research project and report. The key person in keeping that project on a steady course was Joan L. Miller, Project Coordinator, whose diligence and involvement in the substance of the first report far surpassed formal responsibilities. Other chief contributors to that report included Irving A. Spergel, Professor of Social Service Administration, William Swenson, Instructor, Social Sciences Collegiate Division, Richard Brail, now Associate Professor at Rutgers University, Barbara Yondorf (all of the University of Chicago); and Dr. Myrna Bordelon Kassel, Director of the Human Services Manpower Career Center of the Illinois Bureau of Employment Security. Graduate students who rendered able assistance in assembling data or preparing tables included R. Samuel Boyd, Jerry Dahlke, Lawrence Goldberg, Leonard Zax, and Gary Kiken. The writer is particularly appreciative of the unfettered opportunities provided by the University of Chicago at its Center for Urban Studies to pursue this subject wherever it might lead. As in any research endeavor, the assumptions, analysis and conclusions reflect the views of the author, who also bears sole responsibility for errors and omissions.

Above all, special thanks are extended to Jack Meltzer, Professor of Social Sciences and former Director of the Center for Urban Studies. The conception of community service, which provides the central frame of reference for the study, has its genesis in the work of Jack Meltzer. Many of the ways outlined in the text, through which an institution of higher learning can become productively involved with community groups in building collaborative, multidisciplinary, client-centered projects, have been tested in the field at the Center for Urban Studies, under his direction. Much that was learned by the writer about community projects stems from these experiences so that, conceptually, he is the authentic parent of the study. More concretely, I am personally grateful for his extraordinarily generous support and counsel over the entire course of the research and for his many perceptive criticisms and suggestions in reading the initial drafts.

D. Gale Johnson, Professor of Economics and former Dean, Division of Social Sciences; Brian J.L. Berry, Professor of Geography; and Robert J. Havinghurst, Professor Emeritus of Education and Human Development (all at the University of Chicago) read selected chapters of the first draft, as did Joel L. Fleishman, Vice-Chancellor for Public Affairs, Duke University; Meyer Weinberg, Coordinator of Innovation and Master Planning of the City Colleges of Chicago; Allan Rosenbaum, Associate Professor of Political Science, University of Wisconsin; and Ruth Barcan Marcus, Professor of Philosophy, Northwestern University. Each offered insights from varied points of view, which were invaluable in clarifying some of the thornier questions. The writer is indebted to each, but none bears any responsibility for aberrations or errors.

Ralph W. Tyler, Director Emeritus of the Center for Advanced Study in the Behavioral Sciences at Stanford, California and Acting Director of the Social Science Research Council, also read the manuscript and has written a special foreword for the book. At one or another time in his extraordinarily productive life, Dr. Tyler has addressed virtually every aspect of education, ranging over the entire spectrum of institutions, contributing new insights and practical solutions to a host of educational problems, whether in inner-city public schools or independent, progressive schools, whether in preschools or postdoctoral institutions, whether in mass testing programs and systems analysis or in the intimate, interpersonal aspects of teacher-pupil relations, whether in functional education for employment or in basic graduate studies in social and behavioral sciences, whether in rural or in urban universities. In short, there is hardly an educational issue discussed in this book that has not benefited, directly or indirectly, from his earlier work. Our debt and respect for that work are boundless.

Finally, over the course of the study, the writer visited many campuses, rural and urban, multiuniversities, developing and established universities, senior colleges and community colleges, new and old, black and white, and talked with numerous faculty members, administrators and local community leaders, most of whom were deeply involved in community service activities. Their experiences and problems helped to shape our approach. Since these dedicated and generous people number in the hundreds, individual contributions cannot be acknowledged here. Nor can those of other officials in government and higher education who were interviewed. Nevertheless, their collective contribution was particularly significant in identifying the issues and formulating the proposals for action later presented.

In the latter context, in setting forth possible lines of action that follow from particular lines of inquiry, the book reveals its origins as a policy planning report for a specific state system, and deliberately so. Our acknowledged and unabashed purpose is to stimulate and set in motion the policy responses appropriate to the needs of the urban poor. In trying to be as concrete as possible, we are often tempted to draw on the Illinois situation for persuasive evidence in defining problems and in illustrating feasible ways to resolve them. The advantages of specificity, in our judgment, often outweigh the risk that the shoe may not always fit every local situation perfectly.

We have also chosen to focus, primarily, on public tax-supported systems of higher education, even though much of the discussion might apply, equally well, to many private colleges or universities, and again, it is a deliberate choice. Seventy percent of all college students attend public institutions of higher learning, including the vast majority of students who are poor and live in large cities. Moreover, state colleges and universities have a long, unequivocal tradition of public service. The issues in dispute, therefore, do not revolve around whether or not public service activities are appropriate to higher education, but rather in what areas, for whom, and how.

Colleges and the
Urban Poor

1

The Search for New Ways to Serve

Universities and colleges serve many purposes and many publics, especially large and intricate, tax-supported, state systems of higher education. The land-grant colleges and teacher training institutes, established after the Civil War to serve an agrarian, rapidly industrializing society, are the progenitors of many public institutions forming the core of state systems. From the time of founding, public service activities, of which "community service" is but one, have been characteristic of most state colleges and universities. The dissemination and application of knowledge has been a sustained, explicit commitment, representing an implicit compact with taxpayers who support the system.

Over the course of the past century, however, as the needs of the larger society have changed, so have public service activities. Mostly, they have grown by accretion. To the original network of services to agriculture, new extension services have been added, incrementally and gradually, to industry, commerce, the professions, and other special constituencies. Students, parents and alumni, farmers, manufacturers, trade associations and unions, state and local governments, federal agencies, the foundations, the media, doctors, lawyers, teachers, crippled children, art and music devotees, and sometimes even neighbors, together comprise a host of discrete, readily identifiable publics directly served by state colleges and universities.

The role and involvement of public institutions of higher learning with still another, probably least-served constituency, the urban poor, are explored in this book. Clearly, the flow of services and traditional extension programs diminish markedly in the precincts of the urban poor. The educational consequences of past social and economic inequities largely account for the narrowing of the stream. And until recently, many colleges and universities have been totally removed from the concerns, often, of their most proximate neighbors.

During the mid-sixties, however, an upsurge of interest in urban problems swept across the campuses, bringing new forms of community service activities. Even before internal and external pressures mounted to a high pitch of intensity, before the colleges were so beleaguered and at times even besieged, a significant core of faculty, students and administrators on many campuses were seriously grappling with social problems outside their walls. Peace, pollution, racism, participation, poverty, and the cities were the issues inside the walls as well.

Seeking to use their skills and energies constructively, a profusion of new, short-term, experimental programs have sprung up on virtually every major campus in the nation. These include a variety of special educational programs for

1

the "disadvantaged," with tutoring and summer programs for youth. Sometimes, they have taken the form of rendering technical assistance and manpower in such projects as Model Cities proposals, addiction clinics, neighborhood health centers, black economic development corporations, or day-care centers. Altogether, this variegated array of small-scale programs might be best described as inventive, ad-hoc attempts to bridge the chasm and to reverse the seemingly inexorable polarization of interest groups by race, class, and age.

However well-intentioned and immediately productive such activities might be, the improvised, finger-in-the-dike approach to urban community service is obviously out of scale with the magnitude, complexity, severity and explosiveness of class and race problems in contemporary cities. Indeed, some of the more hastily designed gestures of concern have already backfired or petered out, while others have absorbed funds and faculty time at a rate that has far outstripped even the lively imagination of their sponsors.

The disparity in the scale of urban problems and the resources of any single, educational institution, in itself, would suggest the need for a systematic analysis of poverty problems relative to the situation, mission and special faculty competencies of a college. But the determination of priorities in the commitment of limited resources has lately become all the more essential as a period of fiscal constraint, tightening budgets, and program retrenchments has settled upon the colleges and the nation. A sober reassessment of purposes, programs, methods and missions is underway in perhaps a quarter of all institutions of higher learning. It is also underway in the many states where master plans and coordinate policies relating to the future growth and direction of the total system are under review. Hopefully, the issues raised and approaches set forth in later chapters will assist in this assessment.

Response with Reform

The twin themes of social responsiveness and institutional reform are intertwined throughout the study. In essence, a renewed vision of community service is presented, a way of proceeding in building collaborative programs with the poor, a way that might be both feasible and effective. Such cooperative, consumer-oriented approaches, however, are seen as take-off points as well for deep-seated improvements within higher education, for long-overdue internal reforms in pedagogy and in the organization of research. Programs for the poor are not viewed as diversionary extensions of services but are rather conceived as feeding into the mainstream of institutional self-renewal in a manner that can enhance its vitality. Because the questions raised are inherently complex and certainly controversial, the links in the long chain of analysis that support this approach are laid out for inspection in this and other early chapters.

The task of interpreting the traditional goals of higher education in contemporary terms is a continuous one, and the proposals advanced here are ultimately directed toward that task. Although its immediate focus is upon the eminently concrete and pressing problems of the poor and upon the current capacities of scholars, educators and students to address them effectively, a longer perspective is recognized.

In advanced industrial nations, where social conditions change more rapidly than in past times and where news is disseminated widely and quickly, the historic sluggishness of mature, social institutions in adapting old functions to current realities becomes increasingly perilous. Civil disorder in cities and on campuses is testimony to the risks inherent in the widening disjunction between established modes and practices and present perceptions.

Although the superficial manifestations of student unrest have subsided, genuine unrest remains. It has mostly taken the form of a continuing search for alternative, more humane, and sometimes deviant life-styles and of socially purposeful quests. Yet, for institutions of higher learning to become totally embroiled in the passions of the street, the fashions of the minute, or the peer culture of youths would be equally perilous and short-sighted. For state colleges and universities to gear up merely to meet present needs would be a futile exercise as well. Scholars and educators are often quick to perceive that short-range responses are soon "overtaken by events."

In contrast, if programs directed toward meeting the needs of the poor are a critical part of institutional and systemic reform, they can provide an authentic way to demonstrate that large-scale organizations in a mass society can function responsively, rationally and equitably. The historic lag in the responses of scholarly communities to the needs of the larger society can be significantly shortened, bringing internal and external transformations.

Productive Role Possible and Necessary

This sanguine stance regarding the potential responsiveness and possible contributions of public higher education towards resolving the most intractable of urban problems is scarcely universal. It has been correctly pointed out that at present "higher educational institutions, in fact, have neither resources nor the political capacity to engage in such activities except on a modest scale."[1] To acknowledge this is very different, however, from foreclosing in advance the likelihood of positive contributions towards social change by individuals, institutions, or state systems. Furthermore, to acknowledge the constraints and to fail to recognize the imperatives of participation by public institutions would also be aberrant.

The conviction that productive involvement is more feasible at this time than in the past arises from a perception of several recent changes within higher education. First, although existing knowledge about the urban system or social problems provides few certain guides to action programs, individual social scientists and educators in professional schools have begun to amass considerable practical experience and skill in dealing with social issues. Second, a significant, if small, number of scholars in varied fields seek the opportunity to test their models and conclusions against actual social behavior in an attempt to resolve persistent problems. Lastly, urban universities and colleges of necessity have a direct stake in resolving or, at least, mitigating the severity of urban problems. All of these factors, in our view, increase the probability of productive involvement in the immediate future.

The conviction that policies and programs responsive to the needs of the poor are essential for public institutions arises from a perception of other changes in higher education. Free inquiry, rational discourse, and humane educational goals have been generously assailed in recent years from both the right and the left. Higher education is caught in the cross fire. Some would build bastions behind which to retreat from the turbulence rocking the cities. Others would open the gates to any and all requests, converting the colleges into service stations for the state or staging grounds for the revolution. Neither stance in our view is defensible. State institutions can and must take the initiative promptly to carve for themselves paths that are both responsive and authentic.

Of late, there has been a spate of books, monographs and essays about the involvement of higher education in public affairs, most of them highly critical. Ranged on a continuum, the opinions at one end would find their most eloquent spokesman in Jacques Barzun or Robert Nisbet. In essence, these men suggest that the "university" disengage itself totally from direct participation in public affairs and concentrate on what it does best, on its proper business of education and discovery, on cultivating rational thought, learning, and the works of the mind. At the other end of the continuum are the views of such vanguard educators as William Birenbaum and Charles Hurst, many faculty and students, and many more antiestablishment writers such as Ivan Illich or Paul Goodman. In the extreme, together they see higher education as the antiquated guardian of the status quo, the epitome of the inequities of the greater society, and they suggest that colleges be swiftly transformed into "agents of social change."

These critics are often thinking of a single kind of institution, an elite university or a black community college, attempting to take its bearings and define its mission with greater precision. When one views the entire range of public institutions of higher education as presently constituted, the plain fact is that state universities and colleges have been "agents of social change" and have sustained a commitment to public service, variously defined, for over half a century. More than one-third of their present lower-division students are enrolled in community colleges, colleges with clearly expressed dual goals of education and community service. Yet, at the same time, the vast majority of their faculty are dedicated chiefly to the discovery or transmission of knowledge. The polarities in the public polemics on the role of higher education, while suited perhaps to a single institution, are inapplicable to diverse and complex state systems. For them the polarities relate largely to the priorities and balance within each of their systems, the quality and direction of its total performance and that of its component institutions relative to specific situations and defined missions.

The Scranton Commission's report on campus unrest is highly critical of eclectic and controversial service activities, burgeoning in higher education since World War II, particularly those that bear little relation to teaching and research, which are viewed as primary missions.[2] It recommends that universities and their faculties divest themselves of dilatory public service commitments. The report, however, goes on to make a further recommendation: "As universities reduce their extraneous service commitments, they must also search for new ways to serve by relating their policies, programs and expertise to pressing local and national problems." The prime objective of this study is to lend assistance in that "search for new ways to serve."

Service, Teaching and Learning

Fundamental to the development of new policies and programs in poverty areas, is the abandonment of the traditional conception of community service as a function separate and distinct from teaching or learning. In fact, this study begins with exactly the opposite assumption, namely, that the most effective and viable community service endeavors are those that grow out of regular educational and scholarly pursuits and that concurrently feed back insights and practical adaptations.

Community service is a rather ambiguous phrase; community and service are both words subject to varying meanings and possible interpretations. For example, the definition of the "community" of a junior college such as Malcolm X in Chicago or the Peralta Colleges in Oakland, California, turns out to be, operationally, "all our black brothers" or perhaps "third-world oppressed peoples." In contrast, the social and geographic boundaries of the actual "community of reference" of a University of California or Illinois are at least statewide, or more precisely for most faculty, their intellectual peers throughout the world. Both kinds of institutions, however, are situated in places, in neighborhoods, in "community" areas, to whose specific needs they must also be responsive. Without launching into a long definitional digression, the approach taken in the context of this study, at least, can be clarified.

For professional educators, community service has become almost a code phrase covering a wide spectrum of special service programs, extension, and adult, noncredit courses. It is generally a residual category under which are traditionally subsumed those numerous conferences, courses, workshops, projects, in-service training programs, and consultative relationships that are directed mostly toward outsiders, the public—indeed, the many discrete publics identified earlier, among whom, presumably, would be included the urban poor.

Although the activities embraced may be extremely varied, they all share a common vision of service as something extrinsic to the day-to-day business of colleges and universities, something apart from the daily essential work of teaching and learning. With such a view, it is no wonder that contentious issues often tend to center on such questions as whether evening courses should be self-supporting or not; whether regular faculty, special extension faculty, or jointly appointed faculty are most likely to produce quality offerings; whether special service programs should be offered at locations off-campus or on-campus; and similar issues.

While these are important and often difficult, practical questions to resolve, it should be immediately apparent from scanning the contents of this book that there is an alternative umbrella under which to consider such issues. It cannot be assumed that enlarging and refining the present pattern of extension and public service activities is necessarily the most effective way to reach into low-income, urban community areas. Experience and even the most casual acquaintance with life in the precincts of the poor argue otherwise, and the very purpose of this study is to explore new pathways. Therefore, it is essential to set this view aside temporarily, and to consider community service de novo, more naively and more literally, as though the phrase did not already have a close association with established patterns of continuing education, extension and outreach.

To adhere to the traditional conception of the mission of higher education as divisible into three separate provinces, education, research and service, is inappropriate, an anachronism. Each has the capacity to reinforce the other; none can be successfully sustained alone in poverty areas. The rhetoric of higher education, in our judgment, has not yet caught up with its best practices.

The search for new kinds of pedagogical programs that challenge the intellect and sensibilities of students often leads to field work and direct service experiences within the framework of regular academic course work. It is hard, for example, to conceive of an adequate teacher training curriculum that does not provide the opportunity for its students to have direct contact with and to become familiar with the life-styles and problems of youngsters of backgrounds different from those of the prospective teacher.

Yet, to view the neighborhoods of the city as "living laboratories" to be studied and manipulated at the whim of the scholar or educator would be to misread the events of the decade grossly. A research or training program in a poverty area that does not engage the active cooperation of its residents and that is not perceived by them as fulfilling a useful purpose seems improbable today. A genuine partnership and a reciprocal relationship is essential to the success of any neighborhood-based program.

Thus, institutions of higher education are not to be viewed as social agencies extending needed services to the poor, as updated versions of Lady Bountiful, albeit in blue stockings or jeans, bestowing favors graciously in the slums. Higher education is ill-equipped to dispense social services and could never hope to meet the vast pool of human needs in poverty areas. Colonialism or tokenism are the epithets reserved by the poor for such favors.

The continued compartmentalization, operationally, of the theoretical, tripartite division of the mission of higher education is a Procrustean Bed, one from which state systems should be released. The maintenance of sharp distinctions tends to produce service programs in poverty areas of a kind recently characterized as "middle-class voyeurism," in short, intellectually and socially sterile adventures.[a]

In summary, this study begins with the assumption that it is no longer a question of whether public institutions of higher education should engage in community service activities but, rather, of how best to proceed in the contemporary world. Since colleges and universities can never substitute for public and private agencies in the delivery of human services on a mass basis or arrogate to themselves the options that ultimately reside in the consumer, the community area and its members, the issues revolve chiefly around appropriate ways to draw upon the special talents, style and resources of the academic community.

By approaching the subject from the standpoint of the pragmatic needs of urban poverty areas first, it is expected that guidelines for a revised vision of community service will emerge. For this reason, an analytic framework within which to explore the capacities and responsibilities of colleges and universities is set forth in Chapters 2 and 3. Granted, there are alternative points of entry to the subject, surely there are few in which the role of higher education is as obscure.

Although educational institutions and public services are most deficient in urban ghettos and poverty areas, similar deficiencies are often found in working-class and middle-income neighborhoods. Consequently, our exploration of the ways in which institutions of higher education might respond to community needs in poverty areas will undoubtedly suggest institutional adaptations and innovations appropriate to a wide variety of community settings.

---

[a]In their critique, Parker Palmer and Eldon Jacobson of the Washington Center for Metropolitan Studies found typical undergraduate "urban-experience" programs "largely unrelated to classroom instruction," and used the phrase "middle-class voyeurism." They suggested closer integration with academic elements through restructuring the curriculum.[3]

Part One:

2 Urban Poverty

Few issues are as strategic to the quality of life in the cities than urban poverty. The problems associated with poverty and discrimination pervade and impede the resolution of virtually all urban issues, whether they be housing, health, jobs, transportation, crime or local government, whether they be largely fiscal, administrative, or environmental. Intractable problems in inner-city schools are inevitably linked with the effects of poverty and discrimination on their students. Thus, it is especially appropriate for state colleges and universities, as part of the public educational continuum, to focus on the community setting of education as well as on the process itself.

Historically, educational achievement and attainment have been closely correlated statistically with the socioeconomic status of a student's family. In 1968, for example, a young person between the ages of 18 and 24 was nine times more likely to be in college if his family income was over $15,000 than if it was under $3,000.[1] Several recent large-scale studies of urban elementary and high schools have underscored the importance of the social setting of the school as a major factor in the educational performance of its pupils. Both the socioeconomic status of the pupils' family and the social composition of the peer group at school have a bearing on educational outcomes that is more significant statistically than any other combination of variables among school systems.[2]

While the importance of the community setting of the school has been corroborated in many studies, there is less agreement about the precise causes of low achievement by disadvantaged students in urban schools segregated by class and race. Policy implications are thus not self-evident, nor are program priorities for improving inner-city schools, such as the question of the primacy of integration or community control. Since poverty is both the inheritance and the legacy of many for several generations, it is often difficult to disentangle its causes from its consequences, and a combination of interrelated, joint causes and joint effects are usually observed.

In contrast, it is easy to see that urban schools, as presently constituted, rarely counteract the educational disadvantages of being born into a poor family in a poor neighborhood. The educational system, from kindergarten through university, has yet to become "the great equalizer of the condition of men, the balance wheel of the social machinery" that Horace Mann, the spiritual father of public education in the United States, envisioned in the nineteenth century.

State colleges and universities sit at the capstone of the public system of education, an elaborate network of elementary and secondary schools, urban, sub-

11

urban and rural, whose great diversity stems largely from its community setting. The role of higher education in poverty areas can only be defined in terms of the performance of the total education system which, in turn, reflects the social, economic, and political climate. Public higher education is intimately linked with both.

This chapter offers background information for identifying the role of higher education in relation to the problems of the urban poor. The extent and nature of poverty are reviewed in their economic dimensions, geographic locale, and social setting. Major stratagems for addressing poverty are outlined in the following chapter, and broad social policy implications are spelled out.

Poverty is usually defined as an economic phenomenon, but its social concomitants are no less important. Both aspects of poverty are significant to educational policy. To live in abject poverty in a rich country is to be an outsider; it is to live of necessity with short-term perspectives and limited options, including educational ones.

The persistence of poverty amid plenty scarcely needs documentation, so prominent and divisive is the issue, so fulsome its treatment in popular and academic journals. But contemporary poverty in the United States has several distinctive characteristics which are singled out for emphasis below.

—Poverty in a rich nation is a question of economic deprivation relative to prevailing, socially defined standards of living.
—Poverty is increasingly an urban phenomenon, and its incidence within cities is heavily concentrated by place and race.
—Prolonged economic deprivation in an affluent society coupled with residential segregation leads to social isolation and a mode of adaption that is self-reinforcing and intergenerational.

The Incidence of Poverty

In simple economic terms, the poor are persons with low incomes; yet the measurement of poverty is exceedingly complex. In the United States, poverty levels of living are defined in two general ways, either as incomes that are low relative to a minimum cost-of-living standard or as the lowest percentile relative to the overall distribution of income shares in the population as a whole. Both methods yield somewhat different conclusions as to the extent of poverty (Appendix A). Since World War II, no change of consequence has occurred in the overall distribution of income shares in the United States. In contrast, as national prosperity and growth during the last two decades have raised all incomes, the number of people with less than minimum, subsistence level incomes has gradually decreased.

Whatever the techniques of analysis, however, a poverty line should be viewed as a socially defined construct and, in the United States, economic deprivation seen as relative to prevailing standards of living. Families with incomes near and above the poverty line generally face the same sorts of problems and living conditions as those below.

An urban household of four was considered poor, according to the sliding minimum cost-of-living standards established by the Social Security Administration, if its annual income was below $3,743 in 1969 or $3,968 in 1970. Such incomes, of course, are well above the averages prevailing in most of the world, even most parts of Western Europe. But they are very much lower than the comparable median of family incomes in the United States, which approximates $9,000, subject to local variations. The Bureau of Labor Statistics has calculated that an annual income of over $9,600 is required by a four-person, urban household to maintain a moderate standard of living. Roughly half the nation's families have incomes below that level and, by that standard, would find the costs of higher education a decided burden.

The number of poor persons declined steadily from 1959, when federal statistics were first compiled, until 1969, at an average rate of 4.9% a year. Nevertheless in 1969, there remained 24.2 million persons in the United States, or 12.2% of the total population, with incomes below the poverty threshold defined by the Social Security Administration.[a]

In 1970, for the first time in a decade, the number of poor persons increased significantly by some 1.2 million persons, bringing the total to 25.5 million or 12.6% of the population.[3] A sharp rise in unemployment was the dominant cause of the increase, but inflation, with higher living costs, also added more elderly people living on fixed incomes to the ranks of the poor.

Just over half of the nation's poor live in metropolitan areas, but 90% of the increase in poor families in 1970 occurred in metropolitan areas. Within metropolitan areas, almost twice as many poor persons live in the central cities than in the suburbs, even though less than half of total metropolitan population now reside in central cities. Outside the South, in the rich industrial states, the metropolitan and central city concentrations of poverty are even more pronounced.[4] For example, if the residency of public aid recipients in Illinois is used as a crude indicator of the parameters of poverty in 1970, about 85% of all beneficiaries lived in the state's nine metropolitan areas; in fact, 70% lived in just one of them, Chicago, and half within its central city (see Tables B-3 and B-4).

Although the high incidence of poverty among blacks, Hispanic-Americans and American Indians is well-known, it would be very misleading to assume that the poor are chiefly nonwhites and that poverty areas are ipso facto the urban ghettos. In actuality, more than two-thirds of the poor in 1970 were white, and only one-third were black. Yet, it is true that a significantly higher proportion of black families than white have very low incomes and do live in segregated neigh-

[a]In 1960, nearly 40 million persons or about 22% of the population were classified as poor by the same standard.

borhoods of central cities. The incomes of one out of three of all black persons fell below the poverty line, while the incomes of only one in ten white persons were similarly low. The proportion of Spanish-Americans, usually classified as white, with incomes below poverty levels was equally high and higher for American-Indians.

From the standpoint of educational policy, however, what is perhaps more important is that the incidence of poverty among urban blacks and whites is somewhat different. According to a recent study of the poor in central cities by the Bureau of the Census, a relatively higher proportion of white poverty is associated with old age while a somewhat higher proportion of black poverty is related to fatherless families.[b] Furthermore, half of the overall increase in the number of the nation's poor in 1970, and virtually all of the net increase among blacks, was accounted for by members of families headed by women.

Throughout the sixties, the number and proportion of black families headed by women appreciated markedly. By 1970, they composed 27% of all black families, over three times the comparable proportion of 7% among white families. Female-headed households are disproportionately overrepresented among the poor, and by themselves, comprised 53% of all black families outside the South with incomes below poverty levels.[5]

Looking more closely at the changing fates and fortunes of differing types of black families as revealed in the 1970 Census, one finds that the income of young couples under 35, living in the North, rose most dramatically during the sixties to average $8,900, close to comparable white incomes when wives worked. But the larger and growing number of black families headed by women remained in deep poverty. Other types of black families in the nation made modest or token gains so that the relative economic status of female-headed families has worsened in comparison with others. In effect, what has happened is that as better educated, upwardly mobile, black families progressed economically during the decade and moved out of depressed neighborhoods, the concentration of problems in the worst central city areas was intensified.

The role of urban educational institutions is particularly crucial since so many of the poor are children growing up in large or fatherless families in central cities. Of the total number of poor persons of all races in the nation, more than two-fifths, or 42.2%, in 1968 were children under the age of 18. Two-thirds of these 5.4 million poor children lived in central cities, and more than half the poor children in central cities were black.[6] The larger the family, the greater the probability that incomes would be low, both in relative and absolute amounts. In 1967, for example, 35% of the nation's poor families had six or more chil-

---

[b]In a survey of poor families living in central cities of metropolitan areas in 1967, the Bureau of the Census reported that about 30% of poor, white families were headed by persons over 64 years old, compared with only 11% of poor black families. In the under-65 category, 40% of poor white families were headed by females while the proportions were reversed among poor black families, where 62% were headed by females.

dren, while families with one child represented only 8.4% of the total.[7] The quality of educational and public services made available to these children and their families in the next decade will determine whether children born in poverty, dependency and often discrimination can find their way out of deprivation.

The close association between formal education and earnings is widely recognized. In 1970, for example, college graduates had a median income of $16,000, which was three times the income of workers with less than a grade-school education.[8] The relationship between formal schooling and access to better jobs and earnings also shows up in poverty statistics. Of families whose heads had completed less than eight years of school, 25% were poor in 1968. Among families whose heads had completed eight years of school, the incidence of poverty was cut in half at 13%. Rates continued downward as formal educational levels rose, to only 2% among families headed by college graduates.[9]

Even though the correlation of educational attainment with occupational and income levels is not completely consistent, especially for nonwhites where racial discrimination is a significant, independent, intervening factor in employment, the lack of an adequate basic education is frequently an absolute and insurmountable barrier to a steady job. In 1966, nearly one-fifth of the nation's nonaged poor families were headed by men or women with less than six years of formal schooling, and three-fourths did not graduate from high school.[10]

The number of years Americans spend in school has been progressively rising, shooting up dramatically in the last decade, and the gap in educational attainment between minorities and whites has been closing.[11] Yet, illiteracy persists and is far more widespread even in urban areas than commonly believed. The federal government estimates that the 8.3% of the population that has not gone beyond fifth grade in school is functionally illiterate.[c] But the amount of formal schooling that a person receives has been found to be a very crude indicator of what he may actually learn.

Several recent studies reveal that many more people than official statistics indicate have literacy problems which are serious enough to impair their daily life. A survey conducted in 1970, asking a cross-section of the population to fill out simplified application forms for such things as Social Security, Medicaid or a driver's license, found that at least 13% and perhaps as high as 24% of all persons over age 16 "lack the reading ability necessary for survival" in our culture.[12] A similar recent survey conducted at Harvard and using unsimplified, standard application forms for employment or automobile licenses found the level of functional illiteracy in the nation to be at about 50% of the total population.[13]

The full extent of illiteracy is unknown, but the extraordinarily high rates of failure among the poor in the preinduction Selective Service mental tests clearly indicate that functional illiteracy is not a problem of the past or confined to

---

[c]Advance reports from the 1970 Census indicate that the number of illiterate persons in the nation declined by 50% between 1960 and 1970 but that the proportion living in southern states rose from 40% in 1960 to 66% in 1970.

backward rural regions. It is common today among youths in urban poverty areas.

Of all young men called up for induction into the Armed Forces in 1968, 8.0% were rejected for failing the mental test, a test of simple skills sufficient to cope with the minimum demands of the Armed Forces and surely therefore of an urban, industrial society. Yet, despite compulsory school attendance until age 16, rates of failure among youths in many central cities tend to be much higher (see Table 2-1). For example, the citywide rate of failure in Chicago was double that of the nation, at 16.6%. In poor neighborhoods, rates tended to be even higher, double again the high citywide rates. On the west side of Chicago, for example, just west of the Circle Campus of the University of Illinois, one in three of all youths called up for induction, or some 35.5% of those examined, could not pass the written mental tests (see Table 2-2). These high city rates contrast sharply with the suburban and downstate rates of failure of one in thirty-three, or only 3%.[d] Rates of failure on physical grounds are much more evenly distributed geographically.

No more clear-cut indicator can be found to illustrate the contrast in the life chances and educational achievement or, more precisely, lack of achievement, of inner-city and suburban youths. How many of the young men rejected attended urban public schools, how many migrated from rural areas is unknown; but all presently need training if they are ever to become self-sufficient. Without literacy, job prospects are almost nil, and there are few realistic alternatives to a life of petty hustling or borderline criminal activity.

In sum, when one examines any specialized set of small area, social statistics in any large metropolis, whether it be life expectancy, infant mortality, illegitimacy, deteriorated housing, unemployment, crime or addiction, a clear geographic pattern emerges. It is a stark pattern of multitudinous and often intense problems, intercorrelated with poverty and distinctly localized. Problems are localized by place, primarily concentrated in a selected number of urban community areas. They are concentrated by race as well, since racial and language minorities are more likely to confront a double liability of both poverty and discrimination.

Urbanization and Metropolitan Disparities

The vast black ghettos and poverty areas characteristic of United States cities have been growing in scale with the outward territorial expansion of metropolitan regions. Massive population movements after World War II accelerated the concentration of social, economic, racial and educational problems in cities but, most of all, in particular districts of each city. Suburbanization has accompanied

---

[d]The average rate of failure on the mental test for Illinois, as a whole, was 7% and is below national averages, which include Southern states with notably deficient rural school systems.

urbanization, and with expansion, internal differences among neighborhoods in metropolitan areas have been accentuated. Not only was the trend towards greater specialization in business locations sustained, but longstanding, socioeconomic disparities in residential districts have also been sharpened.

Advance reports from the 1970 Census indicate unequivocally that two powerful, long-prevailing, demographic trends, namely, urbanization and rapid suburban growth, continued unabated throughout the sixties, perpetuating segregated residential patterns. Since it is very doubtful that the exodus of white families to the suburbs will be reversed, a review of what has been happening might be useful.

By 1970, 70% of the nation's population lived in metropolitan areas and more than half outside their central cities. While the total population in the United States grew by 13.3%, the population in the suburbs of 230 metropolitan areas increased much faster, by some 63.4%, about the same rate as in the fifties (64.3%). Population growth in central cities, however, flagged noticeably during the period at 11.7%, a rate of growth that compares with 20.1% during the fifties. Indeed, some of the older central cities experienced a net loss in total population and almost all, a significant net loss of white, middle-class residents.

Huge population shifts occurred during the sixties which the figures on aggregate population changes do not reveal. In fact, were it not for the increase in central cities of blacks and other minority groups or immigrants, the relative decline in their total population would have been even more precipitous. For example, the Census Bureau estimates that in just the 67 largest metropolitan areas, those of more than half a million in population, 12.5 million whites moved out to the suburbs during the decade while 3.4 million blacks, in turn, moved into their central cities.[14] With the massive exodus of white families to the suburbs, the territorial expanse of black ghettos was enlarged, densities reduced, and older housing was abandoned as better housing became available to those who could afford it.

Although a growing number of black families also moved to the suburbs during the sixties, the suburban towns, with few exceptions, remained predominantly white enclaves because of the more rapid, simultaneous, outmigration of white families. The net result was that blacks in suburbs still represented only 4.5% of the total suburban population in 1970 as compared with 4.2% in 1969.[15] Preliminary reports indicate that blacks have largely settled in innerrim towns, contiguous with older ghettos, or in the miniature ghettos of suburban counties, with only a trickle moving into otherwise white neighborhoods.

Tallying the resultant changes by race in all metropolitan areas by 1970, 54.09 million whites, or 58% of total white metropolitan population, lived in suburbs, and 39.8 million lived in central cities. In contrast, 2.57 million blacks or 16% of total black metropolitan population, lived in suburbs while the vast majority of 12.48 million blacks lived in central cities.[16]

Although urbanization and suburban growth, per se, are scarcely newsworthy,

Table 2-1
Indicators of the Quality of Life in Seventeen Largest Metropolitan Areas

Metropolitan Area	Per Capita Income, 1967[a]	Percent of Labor Force Unemployed 1968	Low Income Households (under $3,000) 1968	Housing Cost[b] 1968	Selective Service Mental Test Rejection Rate 1968	Infant Deaths per 1,000 Live Births 1967
New York	$3,868	3.0%	14.3%	$2,727	12.0%	22.7
Los Angeles	$4,029	4.7%	16.5%	$2,278	7.0%	19.9
Chicago	$4,014	3.0%	11.4%	$2,617	11.0%	24.4
Philadelphia	$3,462	3.2%	13.9%	$2,222	11.0%	24.4
Detroit	$3,872	3.8%	9.8%	$2,208	8.0%	22.7
Boston	$3,371	2.5%	9.3%	$2,832	7.0%	19.4
San Francisco	$4,075	4.8%	17.5%	$2,578	6.0%	19.3
Washington	$3,641	2.7%	9.4%	$2,406	15.0%	20.7
Pittsburgh	$3,441	4.4%	14.8%	$2,032	5.0%	21.4
St. Louis	$3,450	3.1%	15.6%	$2,315	6.0%	24.0
Cleveland	$3,645	3.5%	12.4%	$2,646	8.0%	21.0
Baltimore	$3,551	3.4%	13.5%	$2,056	10.0%	23.1
Houston	$3,480	3.3%	17.8%	$1,927	10.0%	21.8
Minneapolis	$3,788	2.4%	11.9%	$2,392	2.0%	19.6
Dallas	$3,729	2.3%	17.1%	$2,005	8.0%	23.2
Cincinnati	$3,454	2.9%	16.8%	$2,272	7.0%	20.5
Milwaukee	$3,656	2.9%	11.0%	$2,584	3.0%	20.1
Buffalo	$3,133	4.0%	13.5%	$2,498	4.0%	22.3
Average	$3,645	3.3%	13.7%	$2,366	8.0%	21.7

[a]Adjusted for cost of living differences.
[b]To house a moderate income family of four.

Metropolitan Area	Suicides per 100,000 Population, 1967	Air Pollution Index, 1966	Reported Robberies per 100,000 Population, 1968	Traffic Deaths per 100,000 Population, 1967	Known Narcotics Addicts/10,000 Population, 1967
New York	7.2	457.5	485	13.3	38
Los Angeles	22.4	393.5	273	24.8	14
Chicago	8.2	422.0	305	17.2	17
Philadelphia	9.2	404.5	115	17.9	7
Detroit	10.4	370.0	378	20.7	12
Boston	7.1	389.0	97	15.6	7
San Francisco	23.5	253.0	377	25.0	9
Washington	8.1	327.5	379	17.4	14
Pittsburgh	8.6	390.0	150	19.0	4
St. Louis	10.2	369.0	220	23.5	4
Cleveland	10.4	390.5	186	15.9	1
Baltimore	8.1	355.0	455	20.1	20
Houston	11.1	233.5	232	4.8	1
Minneapolis	9.9	257.0	167	20.5	3
Dallas	9.8	178.0	86	25.3	1
Cincinnati	10.1	325.5	75	14.8	n.a.
Milwaukee	10.0	301.5	62	17.1	2
Buffalo	6.1	260.0	107	19.2	14
Average	10.6	331.5		19.4	10

n.a. = not available

Source: Martin V. Jones and Michael J. Flax, *The Quality of Life in Metropolitan Washington, D.C.: Some Statistical Benchmarks*, The Urban Institute, Washington, D.C.

Table 2-2
Illinois Selective Service System, Registrants Examined for Induction, 1969

Location of Local Board	Total Examined	Total Qualified for Induction	Total Rejected		Reason for Rejection							
					Mental		Physical		Mental and Physical		Moral	
			Number	%	Number	%	Number	%	Number	%	Number	%
City of Chicago	20,885	10,517	10,368	49.6	3,477	16.6	6,144	29.4	577	2.8	170	.8
West-Side of Chicago*	1,562	664	898	57.5	558	35.7	240	15.4	80	5.1	20	1.3
Cook County, outside Chicago	9,837	6,104	3,733	37.9	308	3.1	3,302	33.6	59	.6	64	.7
Downstate, not including Cook County	32,420	22,437	9,983	30.8	971	3.0	8,548	26.4	244	.8	220	.7
ILLINOIS Total	63,142	39,058	24,084	38.1	4,756	7.5	17,994	28.5	880	1.4	454	.7

*Composed of Selective Service System Offices 14, 16, 53, 55, 57, 58, 59.

Source: Selective Service System, Illinois Headquarters.

having persisted for decades and throughout the world, the huge scale and social impact of recent population changes are often unappreciated. In a sense, the problems of many of the urban poor may be viewed as the second and third generational result of rural poverty neglected in the past, easily neglected so long as the poor were dispersed in rural counties. For the new generations, born in dense, segregated urban slums, however, poverty was transformed, and their problems are of a distinctively different order and magnitude.

Between World War II and 1967, upwards of 22 million people in the United States migrated from rural areas to the cities seeking opportunity or driven off the land by technological advances in agriculture. The permanent farm population in the nation was reduced by the late sixties to between 5% and 6% of the total population.

Incomes and living conditions improved for most of the urban immigrants, but those who were black and equipped with only primitive educational and vocational skills fared least well. They settled predominantly in the central cities of large, industrial states. This wave of migration, it should be noted, is comparable in size to the wave of European immigration between 1890 and 1920, a period in which 23 million foreign immigrants poured into the cities. As recently as 1940, for example, 77% of all blacks in the United States lived in the South, but by 1970, the comparable proportion was only 53.2%, most of whom, by then, resided in urban areas.[17]

The urbanization of racial minorities proceeded at a somewhat faster rate than that of the white population. In 1910, 73% of the blacks in the country lived in rural areas with less than 2,500 inhabitants, but by 1960, the percentage was precisely reversed with 73% living in urban areas. In 1910, 52% of the nation's total white population lived in rural areas and by 1960, 70% resided in urban areas.[18]

Since 1960, contrary to earlier reports that the migration of blacks to northern cities and states was slackening, the Census Bureau reports that southern blacks streamed north at a rate that was nearly comparable to the high levels of the two previous decades. More than three-fourths of the 1.4 million black migrants who came from the South during the sixties settled in only five large states and mostly in the central cities. New York gained 396,000 black migrants, California gained 272,000, and New Jersey, Illinois and Michigan each gained about 120,000 persons.[19]

The geographic pattern of both intrametropolitan settlement and industrial growth in the last three decades has made assimilation and social mobility exceedingly difficult for poorly educated inner-city residents. Employment growth in blue-collar, trade and lower eschelon service jobs has been most rapid in suburban towns, while unskilled workers have largely settled in older city neighborhoods in housing vacated by upwardly mobile families. Racial discrimination in housing and restrictive suburban zoning perpetuated and reinforced these settlement patterns. Many of the economically depressed and segregated neighborhoods in central cities and older towns are presently extremely isolated, socially and geographically, from the mainstream of opportunity. The sheer size of cities today, coupled with inadequate public transit, has contributed to the isolation. As a result, ports-of-entry have largely become permanent anchorages for the poorest families, and living conditions in these impacted areas contrast sharply with those elsewhere.

The disparities among the neighborhoods and community areas that compose city and suburb are enormous in such things as income, safety, health, schools, accessibility, housing quality, social cohesiveness, race or ethnicity. These differences, drawn mostly along color and class lines, have proven to be formidable barriers to cooperation among neighboring communities and have reinforced inequalities in the fiscal capacities of contiguous cities and counties. The principal loci of social problems are the older neighborhoods of central cities and industrial towns, where costs of public services are highest and growing. Yet, where problems and needs are greatest, the resources to address them are often least adequate.

The chaotic and anachronistic boundaries of local governmental jurisdictions partially account for this, but the administration of particular functional programs, such as in health, housing or education, also contribute to the diffusion of responsibility. To cite an easy example, the differences in per pupil expenditure among the many separate school districts in metropolitan areas are immense. In the suburban ring of Chicago, for example, in 1969, one district spent $1,245 per pupil, almost three times more than in another district which spent $445 per pupil. Furthermore, within the city of Chicago, there was also a wide spread in the actual per pupil expenditures at different schools, varying as much in 1969 as between $263 and $653 per pupil within the single system.[20] The chief prevailing disparities, however, are those between central city and suburban ring and between black poverty areas and middle-class white neighborhoods within both.

The fragmentation of governmental authority in metropolitan areas and the crazy-quilt pattern of overlapping functional jurisdictions have a particularly pernicious effect in poverty areas. Here, coordinated and comprehensive public services are vital; yet responsive local programs are often stymied for lack of both resources and clear responsibility.

In toto, there are 81,242 separate units of local government in the United States. In 1967, Illinois alone contained 6,453 and had the unenviable distinction of leading the nation with more units of local government than any other state, while the Chicago metropolitan area shared a similar distinction among the cities of the nation.[e] The chief agents of fiscal inequities among community

---

[e]The 6,453 separate local governmental entities in Illinois were about 29.1% higher than in the next highest state, and approximately 296% higher than in the average state. The numbers are higher, but the situation is nationwide. In Illinois, there are 102 counties, 1,256 municipalities, 1,432 townships, 1,350 school districts, 2,313 special districts. In the Chicago Metropolitan Area, residents live in 6 counties with 250 municipalities, 114 townships, 327 school districts, and more than 400 other special districts, all providing a variety of services.[21]

areas are these fragmented, local governmental units, but the other functional agencies operating within metropolitan areas compound the inequities. Modernization of administration has been opposed largely by those with vested interests in preserving the social and political differences among communities, including state legislatures with rural and suburban biases.

The impact on schools and, most recently, on urban commuter colleges of persistent socioeconomic disparities among community areas has been profound. Schools whose students are exclusively poor or black are generally deficient schools with lower-than-average pupil achievement. The public school system of Chicago, for example, is presently the most segregated of any major northern city (see Tables 2-3 and 2-4). Average juniors in high schools located in poverty areas—and these are the students who have not dropped out—are reading and computing at elementary school levels of competence (see Table 2-5). Thus, although educational attainment, as measured by number of years in school, has risen steadily for all pupils everywhere in the nation, including Chicago, and most rapidly for black students, actual teaching and learning in inner-city schools have woefully lagged in every major city.

Three policy implications for urban public colleges may be drawn immediately from the educational effects of prevailing segregated living patterns. First, it is obvious that the graduates of deficient urban high schools, who enroll in public colleges, need strong compensatory programs and new pedagogical approaches if they are to progress and if open-admissions policies are not to become another cruel hoax.

Second, it is also evident that as opportunities for higher education expand in metropolitan areas, a de facto segregated system of public colleges is likely to emerge if area boundaries are drawn in conformance with existing city and town-

Table 2-3
Pupil Segregation in Ten Largest School Districts in United States, 1968

City	Percentage of Pupils who are Black	Percentage of Blacks in Schools where Fewer than Half the Pupils are Black	Percentage of Blacks in Schools where More than 99 Percent of the Pupils are Black
Chicago	52.9	3.2	75.9
New York	31.5	19.7	26.4
Los Angeles	22.6	4.7	52.1
Detroit	59.2	9.0	37.7
Philadelphia	58.8	9.6	43.5
Houston	33.3	5.3	79.2
Miami	24.3	12.4	72.7
Baltimore	65.1	7.7	66.0
Dallas	30.8	2.1	53.1
Cleveland	55.9	4.8	67.8

Source: U.S. Department of Health, Education and Welfare.

Table 2-4
Racial Composition of Chicago Public Schools, 1969

Pupils	% White	% Black	% Other
Elementary	38.6	55.9	6.5
Secondary	48.1	48.0	3.9
Average	41.0	53.9	5.1
Teachers			
Elementary	62.6	36.9	0.5
Secondary	72.2	27.3	0.5
Average	65.5	34.0	0.5
Administrative			
Personnel	74.4	25.1	0.5

Source: Board of Education, City of Chicago.

ship lines, as has been customary for community colleges. The racial and social composition of the student bodies of community colleges and of senior commuter colleges, to a lesser degree, already reflect residential segregation in the very states that have been most alert to providing equality of access to the poor. The drift toward a de facto segregated system of urban public colleges is imminent in such states as California or Illinois.[f]

The third policy implication, somewhat more problematic, is that the prospects for traditional higher education among the children of the abysmally poor remain slim, as they have been historically. The likeliest escape route from the slum for the increasingly isolated, hard core of the poorest families today is not the B.A. If the thrust of public universities in poverty areas were directed toward the reforms of those institutions and systems that perpetuate dependency and isolation and with which they are already involved as educators and scholars, their energies might be well spent.

Poverty Areas

While impoverished families live in many places, the focus here is upon those bleak, disorderly tracts in every large city inhabited primarily by the poor and near poor. Whether predominantly black, the most numerous; or American-Indian, the most isolated; or Appalachian white, the most transient; or Hispanic-American, the most seemingly foreign; all urban poverty areas share some common characteristics. The chief one, obviously, is an unstable and inadequate income flow. Meager earnings and widespread unemployment are typically also

[f]See Chapter 6 (Segregation) for a discussion of the emergence of de facto segregation among public colleges and Tables 6-2, 6-4, 6-5 and 6-6.

Table 2-5

Achievement Test Scores and Selected Student Characteristics, Public High Schools, City of Chicago, 1968-1969

Chicago Public High Schools	DAT Test Scores[1] 11th Grade		Race and Language		Students Enrolled 9/26/69	Enrollments and Graduations		Graduates' Plans[7]	
	Median Percentile Rank[2]	National Grade Level Equivalent[3]	% Students in Major Racial Group[5]	% Students for whom English is a Second Language		Dropout Rate 1968-69[6]	No. of Graduates 1968-69	% to College	% to Work
Cregier Vocational	5	below 8a[4]	98B	.7%	752	21.9%	71	47.2	36.1
Cooley Vocational	10	below 8a	97B	0%	667	20.5%	68	39.3	54.1
Crane	10	below 8a	98B	.4%	3279	18.4%	340	60.3	27.8
Marshall-3 campuses[8]	10	below 8a	99B	0%	5207	15.7%	572	53.3	31.7
Carver	15	below 8a	100B	0%	1145	13.7%	147	61.2	32.6
DuSable	15	below 8a	100B	0%	3258	10.3%	474	52.8	34.3
Englewood	15	below 8a	100B	0%	2932	9.9%	422	61.2	30.6
Farragut	15	below 8a	92B	1.9%	2946	26.2%	380	66.3	25.9
Flower Vocational	15	below 8a	99B	.1%	1187	11.1%	214	41.6	36.7
Forrestville	15	below 8a	100B	0%	1602	18.4%	230	67.0	23.1
Parker-2 campuses[8]	15	below 8a	100B	0%	2144	18.1%	302	64.5	20.9
Phillips-2 campuses[8]	15	below 8a	99B	.3%	3700	8.4%	375	56.5	31.3
Simeon Vocational	15	below 8a	99B	0%	1563	11.1%	114	34.6	50.5
Waller	15	below 8a	66B	11.9%	2258	18.4%	272	45.3	42.0
Westinghouse Voc.	15	below 8a	98B	.6%	1788	12.5%	67	51.7	34.5
Calumet	20	below 8a	99B	0%	2964	8.6%	480	72.2	17.6
Harrison-2 campuses[8]	20	below 8a	52B	29.5%	3216	20.3%	348	43.5	42.4
Hirsch	20	below 8a	100B	.2%	2026	6.0%	348	71.6	20.6
Hyde Park	20	below 8a	99B	.2%	1389	5.8%	375	55.4	14.5
Tilden	20	below 8a	48B	6.8%	2539	17.2%	312	38.2	29.0
Wells	20	below 8a	45W	24.4%	1971	14.2%	292	34.2	30.9
Dunbar Vocational	25	8b-9a	99B	0%	2484	5.4%	294	38.4	49.5
Harlan	25	8b-9a	99B	0%	3475	6.6%	569	71.8	17.4
Harper	25	8b-9a	62B	.9%	1901	6.4%	349	43.7	45.7
Orr	25	8b-9a	52W	11.7%	1787	18.1%	200	46.4	42.2
Richards Vocational	25	8b-9a	75W	11.6%	730	13.2%	96	20.2	38.2
Spalding Spec. Ed.	25	8b-9a	51B	0%	605	.2%	58	48.2	17.9

Table 2-5 (cont.)

Chicago Public High Schools	DAT Test Scores[1] 11th Grade		Race and Language		Enrollments and Graduations			Graduates' Plans[7]	
	Median Percentile Rank[2]	National Grade Level Equivalent[3]	% Students in Major Racial Group[5]	% Students for whom English is a Second Language	Students Enrolled 9/26/69	Dropout Rate 1968-69[6]	No. of Graduates 1968-69	% to College	% to Work
Tuley-2 campuses[8]	25	8b-9a	49W/50PR	34.5%	2900	15.6%	377	43.8	41.14
Austin	30	9a	73B	.8%	3000	13.8%	532	61.4	26.1
Chicago Vocational	30	9a	80B	.5%	3689	9.9%	590	43.2	38.8
Prosser Vocational	30	9a	93W	4.8%	1385	11.0%	200	36.9	39.5
Chicago Average	35	9a							
Jones Vocational	35	9a	63W	7.0%	998	3.5%	416	17.7	69.1
Kenwood	35	9a	64B	.7%	1533	5.0%	No Sr. Class in 1968-69		
Lake View	35	9a	76W	6.3%	2626	13.4%	392	52.6	33.0
South Shore	35	9a	90B	1.5%	2665	7.2%	410	79.2	15.0
Washington	35	9a	98W	.8%	1825	6.4%	313	41.7	37.7
Bowen	40	10a	70W	5.5%	3851	6.6%	717	65.5	24.8
Gage Pk.-2 campuses[8]	40/20	10a	81W	5.0%	2529	10.3%	425	46.3	39.3
Kelly-3 campuses[8]	40	10a	99W	8.0%	2788	9.9%	495	38.6	48.3
Kelvyn Park	40	10a	92W	3.4%	1822	11.1%	274	50.9	40.2
Roosevelt	40	10a	82W	1.4%	2017	7.1%	412	61.6	27.0
Schurz	40	10a	95W	4.0%	4540	10.2%	785	52.9	35.7
Steinmetz	40	10a	99W	6.9%	2804	6.5%	482	55.0	32.8
Fenger-3 campuses[8]	45	10a-10b	64W	.9%	4094	8.0%	731	55.7	38.1
National Average	50	11a							
Amundson	50	11a	93W	8.1%	1900	7.3%	387	61.6	25.7
Foreman	50	11a	97W	.6%	1910	4.1%	360	77.1	19.3
Hubbard	50	11a	99W	.1%	2488	6.5%	415	52.8	39.0
Kennedy	50	11a	91W	1.1%	3682	6.2%	772	51.0	35.7
Morgan Pk-2 campuses[8]	50	11a	58W	0%	2674	6.4%	470	63.6	24.0
Senn	50	11a	74W	14.8%	3292	10.1%	602	64.7	13.3
Lindblom-Selective Admissions	55	11a	94B	2.3%	1951	3.4%	360	78.9	12.0

Bogan	60	above 11a	99W	.3%	2721	2.0%	595	55.1	34.9
Taft-2 campuses[8]	60	above 11a	99W	0%	3238	3.0%	599	70.5	19.3
VonSteuben	60	above 11a	80W	4.2%	1498	3.5%	288	91.8	3.4
Mather	65	above 11a	98W	.5%	2110	.5%	522	89.2	6.0
Sullivan	65	above 11a	95W	2.0%	1907	6.6%	378	88.7	7.2
Lane-Selective Admissions	75	above 11a	87W	0%	5055	4.4%	1034	81.2	7.7

Source: Chicago Board of Education.

1. Test: Differential Aptitude Test, Form M, Composite Score for Verbal Reasoning and Numerical Ability (DAT).

2. Test scores for Chicago are expressed as the school's national percentile rank on the standardized reading test for Juniors (11th grade). A 30 percentile rank indicates that 29 percent of schools nationally are below that particular school in the test scores and 70 percent are above it.

3. "National Grade Level Equivalent" indicates that the average first semester junior in a particular high school is scoring at a level equal to the average student in the grade level indicated. For example, at Amundson High School, the average 11th grader is scoring at the same level as the average 11th grader nationally, while at Austin High School, the average 11th grader is scoring at the level of the average 9th grader nationally. A precise grade level equivalent cannot be assigned to those whose grade level falls below 8th nor above 11th grade level. Chicago high school median scores have been converted to national grade level equivalents using the test norms published by the test publisher.

4. a = 1st semester; b = 2nd semester.

5. B = Black; W = White; PR = Puerto Rican.

6. "Dropout rate" indicates the percentage of the student body who left public high school between September 1968 and June 1969, before graduation or completion of a program of study for any reason other than transfer out of school or death.

7. These figures indicate the plans expressed by students; the number actually enrolling in college is not known.

8. Data for the ten high schools which have one or more branch campuses have been aggregated. However, the significant differences in the racial composition and the number for whom English is a second language in the following five schools are noteworthy.

High School and Branch(es)	Students 9/26/69	% Major Racial Group	% Students for Whom English is 2nd Language
Harrison	2759	57B	21.5
Froebel Br.	457	81W	77.8
Tuley	2038	49W	not given by campus
Sabin Br.	862	50PR	
Gage Park	1886	84W	4.9
Branch	643	74W	5.1
Fenger	3010	66W	.5
Curtis Br.	851	59W	1.7
West Pullman Br.	233	56W	.4
Morgan Park	2448	55W	—
Clissold Br.	226	94W	—

at the center of a constellation of other problems. Deteriorating housing, high rates of crime, delinquency and addiction, early death, chronic disability and high rates of psychosis, family instability and illegitimacy, deficient schools and low educational achievement are the frequent handmaidens of poverty.

On the other hand, each urban slum has unique characteristics, reflecting its geographic situation and the cultural heritage, life styles, values, and priorities of its inhabitants. Some of the levers crucial to social change and healthy community development reside in the cultural distinctiveness of each group and neighborhood.

In describing adverse living conditions in the urban slum, it is feasible and often customary to draw a statistical portrait of problems, field by field, item by item. Such quantitative portraits are frequently used to diagnose the problems of the slum and to appraise the policy stratagems seemingly appropriate to resolving these problems. Health planners, for example, customarily define the problems of the urban poor in health terms, such as reducing infant mortality rates or the incidence and fatality of preventable diseases. Urban planners tend to identify problems in physical terms, deficient housing, public facilities, open space, and transportation. Police or fire departments use a variety of high crime and fire rates. Social workers focus most often on family and personal difficulties or sometimes on community institutions and group processes. Educators perceive the problems of the slum in terms of school performance, low achievement rates, high dropout rates, vandalism of school property, low college-going rates and the like.[22]

One could choose any Model Cities neighborhood in the nation and catalog its deficiencies. On the west side of Chicago, for example, due west of the Circle Campus and the medical school of the University of Illinois, one finds average rates of unemployment, public assistance, crime and delinquency that are more than 2 1/2 times those in the city as a whole. The incidence of fire is nine times the citywide rate. Infant mortality is twice that in middle-class neighborhoods. Almost half of all live births, or 45.5%, are illegitimate as compared with a statewide illegitimacy rate averaging 10%, with 4% among whites and 35% among blacks. As we have seen, one in three youths called up for induction into the Armed Forces is functionally illiterate. Even though small-area data are poor and often unreliable, it is not difficult to verify a tangle of pathology.[g]

To rely on such a statistical grid, describing poverty areas exclusively in terms of specific functional deficiencies, and to formulate planning objectives accordingly, however, is to risk letting some of the essential dynamics of slum life slip through the grid. For example, the convergence of problems in poverty areas

---

[g]Rates cited here are computed from data collected from local agencies such as Police Department, Fire Department, Selective Service Headquarters, Department of Health, etc. Boundaries of each agency's jurisdiction vary so that data are not strictly comparable geographically. Rates were calculated for the largest jurisdictional unit falling totally within the community areas of the west side and should be viewed as indicators.[23]

produces a cumulative stress; the piling up of troubles leads to despair and feel-ings of alienation and powerlessness characteristic of sustained poverty and often interpreted as low motivation. Likewise, in resolving interlocking problems, sepa-rate functional programs should be mounted in tandem so that their combined effect is of sufficient critical mass to dislodge existing patterns. Moreover, by formulating policy objectives in conformance with traditional, professional divisions-of-labor, one of the foremost problems is likely to slip through the net. That is the delivery system itself, the fragmented, unsatisfactory and unrespon-sive way that public and private services are made available to the poor. Most important, however, by focusing primarily on deficiencies, it is easy to overlook the reservoir of strength indigenous to the neighborhood which can be enlisted in programs of self-development. For example, while 17.8% of the families resid-ing in the west side area described above had incomes below official poverty levels of near $3,700 for a four-person household in 1969, another 28% of the families of comparable size living in the neighborhood had incomes of $10,000 or more. Because of racial discrimination in housing, most black ghettos in large cities are exceedingly complex socially. High or middle-income families and up-wardly mobile, working-class families often live in close proximity to the social disorganization typical of the slum.

In defining its role in poverty areas, higher education must not fall into the same trap, limiting itself solely to finding ways to increase the enrollment of low-income or minority students. This is an essential but by no means sufficient objective, since even with additional supports, few of this generation's most deprived youths are likely to seek enrollment in traditional colleges. As we shall see in later chapters, there are other key points of entry into the cycle of pov-erty, and a larger role can be conceived in the context of promoting community development.

Two kinds of groups, broadly speaking, inhabit the slums, the fallouts of our competitive urban society, and another larger group, who, for a variety of rea-sons, have never had a chance to compete on equal terms, much less fall by the way. The latter group is composed of relatively stable working-class families who may have meager incomes but whose value orientation is closely allied with that of the middle class. The likeliest immediate candidates for higher education are to be found among their progeny. In contrast, the behavior of the former group corresponds to that described by Oscar Lewis as "the culture of poverty" or, in the terminology of Gunnar Myrdal, the "underclass."

Thus, the urban slum is, first, the haven of failure, of the fallouts, the drop-outs, and the pushouts. Their problems are rarely self-correcting, but rather self-reinforcing, contagious within the family and passed on as a grim legacy to their heirs. Typically, they result from a series of frustrations and repeated defeats at each stage of the life cycle, in the family, in schools, and in work places. To design programs that single out one or another aspect of their problems as, for example, their health, poor work habits, or presumed ignorance, is to risk having the good effects of that program washed out by other concurrent problems. Such has been the actual experience of many recent, pilot programs in inner-city schools.

The second, broad and overlapping category of slum residents is composed of those who because of low incomes and the structure of social institutions are denied access to genuine opportunity. They include a disproportionately high number of racial and language minority groups and other newly arrived, urban residents, rural-whites, unskilled foreigners, and sometimes the second generation of immigrants and the working poor. Although their incomes may rise above officially defined poverty thresholds, their options are, nevertheless, effectively constrained. Endowed with limited family and community resources, a host of institutional obstacles lie in the path of achievement, including racial and language barriers, inferior schools, and the series of bureaucratic, inflexible and insensitive public agencies on which they are dependent, as the middle class is not, for lack of money to go elsewhere. Add to these the pathology of slum life that daily confronts them personally. The street smart and ingenuity of the child of the inner city in dealing with drug addicts, prostitutes, shakedowns and police harassment are testament to the creative, adaptive talents with which many are richly endowed (and which our present educational system fails to develop). That so many have succeeded in getting decent jobs and providing for their children can be credited mostly to their personal vitality, tenacity and resourcefulness. The approach to community service advocated in Chapter 6 builds upon the healthy forces to be found in every poverty area as means to reduce pathology and bring positive social changes.

3 Poverty Policies

It is ironic and perhaps characteristic of the United States that the determination to make a frontal assault on poverty should have gained a consensus in the mid-sixties, a time in which economic conditions were improving markedly. Between 1961 and 1967, for example, the Gross National Product adjusted for price changes increased at an average annual rate of 6.5%, as compared with a sluggish annual growth rate of 2.4% between 1953 and 1957. Similarly, the percentage of families in the United States with incomes under $3,000 in constant 1965 dollars, had declined from 29.9% in 1950, to 20.3% in 1960, to 16.5% in 1965 (Appendix A). There is logic, however, in the seeming irony and in the emergence of a collection of new poverty stratagems.

Shifting Stratagems

By definition, to be poor is to have a low income. Since wages or salaries earned through employment are the predominant and preferred mode of income distribution in the United States (about 80% of the total), the basic national strategy for reducing poverty for decades has been to aim for full employment and economic expansion. When Franklin Roosevelt spoke of "one-third of a nation ill-housed, ill-clothed, and ill-fed," (now, about one-eighth of a nation), it was to herald an antidepression policy. The unspoken assumption was that if the economy were in full gear, incomes would be sufficient to meet most human needs. Of course, it was acknowledged that some persons could not work—the aged, the disabled, female heads of households with young children, to cite a few, and then there was also always temporary, "frictional" unemployment between jobs. The social insurances and public assistance programs were enacted to provide for these presumed contingencies and to supply a minimum subsistence, even if meager in amount, cumbersome and sometimes inequitable in administration.

During the late sixties, however, a period of unprecedented, sustained economic growth, and of tight, urban labor markets, it became apparent that a significant core of unemployment remained. This unemployment was singularly unresponsive to economic growth and persisted in spite of job vacancies. Low skills, deficient education, poor health, inadequate job market information, racial discrimination, family problems, geographic immobility and other formidable obstacles often stood between the worker and the job. Some of these are what economists call "structural" employment problems.

31

In addition, it was found that nearly one-fourth of all persons in metropolitan areas classified as poor according to federal standards based on minimum subsistence levels, lived in families in which the head of the household worked throughout the year but earned very little. Furthermore, there was little prospect that nearly half of all persons with low incomes could become economically self-sufficient by working. In 1968, for example, it was estimated that of impoverished persons living in metropolitan areas, 18.3% were elderly, 4.5% were disabled males under 65, and 23.7% were females under 65 with young children.[1] Since then, the ballooning of welfare rolls has been caused mostly through the addition of mothers and their dependent children.

There was no escaping the fact that, although a full employment and growth strategy was essential, it was insufficient by itself to eliminate poverty even among able-bodied workers. In strictly economic terms, poverty persisted amid plenty because the earning capacities of many individuals were insufficient to support an adequate standard of living, as socially defined. Reforms in the systems of public assistance and social insurances were needed, and several proposals have been under consideration in the Congress. More significant in terms of the role of educational institutions, however, are the policy strategems that emerged during this period of tight labor markets, aimed primarily at raising the productivity of impoverished individuals. An aggregation of new programs was devised, directed ultimately toward human resources and community development.

To put it another way, the Employment Act of 1946 was directed toward the goal of full employment, toward an adequate total supply of jobs, a fundamental precondition to reducing poverty. The objectives of the new policies, however, were to reduce the obstacles that for many blocked access to those jobs and perpetuated poverty and dependency. In probing the roots of hard-core unemployment, underemployment, and intergenerational poverty, attention shifted to two main fronts, to barriers in the job market itself and to the characteristics and living conditions of the poor.

With the shift of emphasis toward human resource and community development programs, education was conscripted, sometimes unwittingly, as an active participant in the war on poverty. This was inevitable because it is generally recognized that the main avenues for developing what economists call human capital are the public schools, higher education, vocational training for youths and adults, and skills gained on the job. The whole gamut of educational institutions from preschool through continuing adult education have a significant if differentiated part to play, including the colleges.

To review, four main groups comprise the vast majority of the poor: (1) the elderly; (2) children living in poor families; (3) employed, adult men and women with low or unstable earnings; and (4) unemployed adult men and women, both within and outside the labor market. Different policies and programs are obviously appropriate for each of these groups to lift them out of poverty, and priorities will vary according to individual circumstances and local conditions. All, however, share a common interim need for supportive public services and a cash flow or its equivalent in goods such as subsidized housing. Almost half of the poor are unlikely ever to become self-supporting because of age or other personal characteristics. For children born into poverty, who alone compose two-fifths of the poor in cities, educational institutions are of prime importance if they are to become self-sufficient and if poverty is to be obliterated in the foreseeable future. Yet the family, peer group, and community setting of childhood are critical in the development of the child and his future achievement. Therefore, even with long-range educational perspectives, community-based programs for parents are also needed, programs designed to strengthen the psychological, cultural, physical, and economic resources of the adult poor. Prime targets for manpower training, in conjunction with allied health, child care, counseling, and other services, are unemployed young men and women and mature women who are the sole breadwinners in the family.

Programs for black teenagers and youths are particularly important. The number of black boys and girls living in central cities shot up rapidly in the last decade, and an even more dramatic future increase is in prospect.[2] From 1960 to 1969, the central city black population between the ages of 16 and 19 increased by 75%, while the comparable number of white teenagers rose by only 14%. Similarly, the youthful black adult population between 20 and 24 years of age rose over 66%, at three times the comparable rate for whites. An accelerated rate of growth can be foreseen in the next decade because of the sharp increase in the number of black and Spanish-American children in cities, coupled with a decline in the number of white children. A disproportionately high number of black and other minority group youths are presently out of school and out of work. Each of these groups occupies a crucial position in terms of sheer numbers and potential long-range payoffs.

Unemployment

Unemployment, undissolved in the solvency of the recent past period of prosperity, was highly concentrated in a comparatively few urban districts and rural counties. It has persisted mostly because of a complex set of obstacles standing between unemployed workers and job vacancies.

Despite very rapid employment and population growth in the suburbs, the actual number of jobs in most central cities has also increased even if at a considerably slower rate.[3] Inadequate transit systems and job market information preclude access to many jobs especially in the suburbs, but other factors may be equally critical sources of persistent central city unemployment and underemployment. Racial discrimination, often in the guise of unnecessarily high job requirements, remains a pervasive obstacle to all but the most menial or occasional jobs. The chief source of unemployment, and that most relevant to educational institutions, stems from the seeming mismatch in the skills of job seekers with existing job vacancies.

Who are the unemployed and underemployed? For the last 15 years, unemployment has been more than twice as frequent among black workers and Spanish-Americans as among whites. It was four times as probable among teenagers as among adult workers; among older workers, higher than average rates also prevailed. In some black urban areas, special unemployment surveys typically have found as many as one in three young people regularly out of work, an unemployment rate that compares with that in the depths of the depression.

Unemployment rates in 1969 provide a particularly good vantage point for observing the sifting out processes of the urban labor market (Tables 3-1, 3-2 and 3-3 illustrate the range of comparable unemployment rates). Composite national and local rates were extremely low, at their lowest level in recent history despite a large increase in the size of the labor force. In 1969, the composite unemployment rate in the United States was 3.5%. It has since risen to 4.9% in 1970, greatly compounding the problems of the poor who are the marginal workers.[a]

Average rates, however, tell us little about those who are unemployed or those who no longer are seeking jobs and have dropped out of the labor force and out of the statistics. Even so, it can be seen (Table 3-2) that the unemployment rate among all married men in the United States, for example, was only 1.4% at the beginning of 1969, a rate indicating little unemployment except that which arises as people change jobs. Yet, despite considerable improvement in the overall employment situation of non-white workers (94% of whom were black), the rate of unemployment among non-white workers was 6%, remaining twice that of all white workers. Among workers between the ages of 16 and 18, the rate amounted to 11.7%.

Official unemployment statistics are often misleading, even though generally interpreted as a reliable barometer of economic health. Average rates for large areas do not reflect the full extent of employment problems in poverty areas of central cities (Table 3-3). For example, thousands of workers, who prefer full-time jobs, are working only part-time. Others are working full-time for less than $65.00 a week or minimum wages, especially female workers in low-skilled occupations. Still others are so discouraged, ill, or alienated that they no longer seek work and are no longer counted in the labor force.

Special surveys in high unemployment areas tell us much more about the scale and nature of joblessness. A survey of the East St. Louis area in 1969, for example, conducted under the auspices of Southern Illinois University, revealed

[a]Composite average rates for Illinois and the Chicago area are characteristically lower than national averages, amounting in 1969, for example, to 2.9% for the State, 3.0% for the Chicago SMSA, and 3.4% for the central city. Unemployment rates by age, sex and race in Illinois and Chicago mirror the national pattern exactly, except that teenage unemployment in the Chicago area was more acute (Tables 3-4 and 3-5).

Table 3-1
Employment Status in United States by Race, Sex, and Age, 1969-70

[Numbers in thousands]						
Employment Status, Sex, and Age	Total		White		Black and Other Races	
	1969	1970	1969	1970	1969	1970
Total, 16 Years and Over						
Civilian labor force	80,733	82,715	71,779	73,518	8,954	9,197
Employment	77,902	78,627	69,518	70,182	8,384	8,445
Unemployment	2,831	4,088	2,261	3,337	570	752
Unemployment rate	3.5	4.9	3.1	4.5	6.4	8.2
Men, 20 Years and Over						
Civilian labor force	46,351	47,189	41,772	42,463	4,579	4,726
Employment	45,388	45,553	40,978	41,093	4,410	4,461
Unemployment	963	1,636	794	1,371	168	265
Unemployment rate	2.1	3.5	1.9	3.2	3.7	5.6
Women, 20 Years and Over						
Civilian labor force	27,413	28,279	23,839	24,616	3,574	3,664
Employment	26,397	26,932	23,932	23,521	3,365	3,412
Unemployment	1,015	1,347	806	1,095	209	252
Unemployment rate	3.7	4.8	3.4	4.4	5.8	6.9
Both Sexes, 16 to 19 Years						
Civilian labor force	6,970	7,246	6,168	6,439	801	807
Employment	6,117	6,141	5,508	5,568	609	573
Unemployment	853	1,105	660	871	193	235
Unemployment rate	12.2	15.3	10.7	13.5	24.0	29.1

Note: Detail may not add to totals because of rounding.
Source: U.S. Department of Labor

Table 3-2
Major United States Unemployment Rate Indicators

Characteristic	January 1969[1]	Annual Averages 1968	1967	1960
Total (all civilian workers)	3.3	3.6	3.8	5.5
Men 20 years and over	2.0	2.2	2.3	4.7
Women 20 years and over	3.5	3.8	4.2	5.1
Both sexes, 16 to 18 years	11.7	12.7	12.9	14.7
White workers	3.0	3.2	3.4	4.9
Nonwhite workers	6.0	6.7	7.4	10.2
Married men	1.4	1.6	1.8	3.7
Full-time workers	2.9	3.1	3.4	([2])
Unemployed 15 weeks or more	.4	.5	.6	1.4

[1] Seasonally adjusted. [2] Not available.
Source: U.S. Department of Labor, Manpower Administration, *Assessing the Economic Scene*, Washington, D.C., 1969.

Table 3-3

Unemployment in the Twenty Largest SMSAs in the United States by Residence, Race, Sex, and Age, 1969

	(Numbers in thousands)			
	Civilian Noninstitutional Population	Civilian Labor Force	Unemployed	Unemployment Rate
Combined SMSAs				
Total	44,042	26,581	906	3.4%
White	38,166	22,861	686	3.0%
Men 20 years and over	16,113	13,509	256	1.9%
Women 20 years and over	18,441	7,556	244	3.2%
Both sexes, 16-19 years	3,612	1,796	185	10.3%
Black and other races	5,872	3,720	221	5.9%
Men 20 years and over	2,297	1,916	73	3.8%
Women 20 years and over	2,880	1,518	75	4.9%
Both sexes, 16-19 years	699	285	72	25.2%
Central Cities				
Total	19,549	11,609	455	3.9%
White	14,865	8,668	274	3.2%
Men 20 years and over	6,259	4,980	121	2.4%
Women 20 years and over	7,398	3,106	96	3.1%
Both sexes, 16-19 years	1,207	582	57	9.8%
Black and other races	4,683	2,941	181	6.2%
Men 20 years and over	1,816	1,501	58	3.8%
Women 20 years and over	2,309	1,212	64	5.3%
Both sexes, 16-19 years	556	229	60	26.1%
Suburbs				
Total	24,493	14,972	451	3.0%
White	23,301	14,193	412	2.9%
Men 20 years and over	9,854	8,529	135	1.6%
Women 20 years and over	11,043	4,450	148	3.3%
Both sexes, 16-19 years	2,405	1,214	128	10.5%
Black and other races	1,193	779	40	5.1%

Source: U.S. Bureau of Labor Statistics.

that no one was employed in almost half, or 48%, of all households in the Model Cities Area.[4] The Bureau of Labor Statistics regularly conducts such surveys in major cities.

Looking at one of them closely, a survey of west side neighborhoods in Chicago, not far from the Circle Campus of the University of Illinois, disclosed that during the year ending June 1969, unemployment rates in these neighborhoods averaged 8.6% (Table 3-4).[b] This was 2 1/2 times the comparable 3.6% rate for the city of Chicago during the months of the survey. In this neighborhood, which is 96% black, almost two out of three, or 63%, of the labor force over 18 had not completed high school as compared with 38% nationally and 57% among black workers. About 17% had less than an eighth grade education, the same percentage as black workers nationally, but of the total labor force in the United States only 10% had received so little formal education.

The high average unemployment rate for the neighborhood, however, masks an even more severe unemployment problem among young people. Almost one out of three teenagers in the area was unemployed, about 31.1%. Comparable national figures were 12.4% among all youths and 24.9% among black youths. Furthermore, an unusually high proportion, one out of four persons who had dropped out of the labor force, reported that they wanted work, a much higher percentage than in the nation as a whole, which was one out of ten in 1966. Health problems across the boards and family responsibilities for potential female workers were the principal reasons stated for no longer actively seeking work (Table 3-5).

The West Side Medical Center, a huge complex of hospitals and schools including the University of Illinois Medical School with its Valley Neighborhood Health Center, the Mile Square Neighborhood Health Center of Presbyterian-St. Luke's Hospital, and the Malcolm X campus of the City Colleges of Chicago with its Allied-Health Institute, are located just to the East, not far from the survey neighborhood. Northeastern Illinois State College and Chicago State College also have outposts near the area, and of course, Circle Campus is the largest nearby university. There is clearly a cluster of problems so extensive that there need be no redundancy in community service programs, and cooperative undertakings would seem appropriate. Similar concentrated employment problems can be found in other neighborhoods in Chicago and in every large city, as illustrated in the thousands of special surveys.

Existing manpower training and related job development programs are miniscule in scale compared with the pool of needs. For example, other manpower surveys of potential workers not actively seeking employment indicate that as many as half of the total adult population living within Model Cities neighborhoods in Chicago might be enlisted in job training programs if proper training facilities and sufficient supportive services were available.[6] Nationally, the number of people needing training for employment was estimated in 1968 at 11 million persons, but the number of training opportunities in major remedial pro-

[b]The west-side area of Chicago in this study consists of East and West Garfield, North Lawndale and parts of the near west side. Statistics for Chicago are for July 1968-June 1969 and are not strictly comparable with those in the other tables which cover January-December 1969.[5]

Table 3-4

Employment in the Chicago Westside Survey Area by Age and Sex, July 1968-June 1969[a]

Age and Sex[b]	Civilian Labor Force	Number Unemployed	Unemployment Rate
Both Sexes			
Total	117,000	66,900	8.6%
16-19	16,900	6,200	31.1%
20-24	15,000	9,500	11.2%
25-44	49,800	33,800	4.8%
45-64	27,200	16,700	2.3%
65+	8,100	800	–
20+	100,000	60,700	5.6%
Household heads	56,500	38,300	3.8%
Household heads 20-64	50,600	33,000	3.4%
Males			
Total	49,900	37,500	7.2%
16-19	7,800	3,200	29.8%
20-24	5,700	4,700	9.6%
25-44	20,500	18,700	3.1%
45-64	12,400	10,300	1.9%
65+	3,500	600	–
20+	42,100	34,200	4.2%
Household heads	35,000	29,400	2.6%
Household heads 20-64	31,800	24,300	2.4%
Females			
Total	67,100	29,400	10.5%
16-19	9,200	3,000	32.6%
20-24	9,300	4,800	12.7%
25-44	29,300	15,100	6.8%
45-64	14,800	6,400	3.0%
65+	4,600	200	–
20+	57,900	26,500	7.3%
Household heads	21,500	8,900	7.3%
Household heads 20-64	18,800	8,700	6.5%

[a]Includes West Garfield, East Garfield, North Lawndale and part of the Near West Side community areas.

[b]No distribution by race because 96 percent of survey area is Negro.

Source: U.S. Department of Labor.

Table 3-5

Reasons Persons in Survey Areas not in Labor Force by Sex, July 1968-June 1969

Reasons Not Looking for Work	Male N=1,900	Female N=9,800
Total reasons		
Number	2,200	11,300
Percent	100.0	100.0
Retirement, age, or school	50.0	14.2
Family responsibilities	–	38.1
Health	36.4	29.2
Looked, but could not find a job	4.5	4.4
Lack of skill, experience or education	4.5	6.2
Other reasons	4.5	8.0

Source: U.S. Department of Labor.

grams came nowhere near that number, amounting to only about 350,000-400,000.[c] The vast need for remedial programs will evaporate only when prime educational institutions in early childhood through youth are improved to the point that they offer what are, in effect, preventive programs.

Education for Tomorrow's Jobs

Looking toward the job markets of the future, the failure of urban schools to teach basic skills successfully to many of their students is ominous. Manpower and vocational training programs will undoubtedly increase in importance, as will the cooperating role of the community colleges. So long as critical major reforms in urban schools are delayed, a second chance to learn must be provided by other institutions.

Continuing technological advances and a growing national appetite for public and private services fed by higher standards of living have created increasing demands in the labor market for highly skilled personnel. Over the course of the last two decades, there has been a steady shift in employment away from goods-producing activities, from farm and blue-collar occupations of all kinds. These trends are expected to continue throughout the seventies.[8]

[c]Some of the listed categories of manpower training needs overlap. Available places in training programs exclude Neighborhood Youth Corps jobs, which amounted to an additional 538,000 in Fiscal 1969.[7]

Professional and technical jobs, which always require higher education, have been increasing more rapidly than other occupational categories and unskilled occupations decreasing at the fastest rate. While the number of workers at the highest occupational levels, professional, technical and managerial, has approximately doubled in the last decade, the shortage of highly skilled personnel is still acute in numerous occupations. The most notable exception is the teaching profession, where supply has overtaken demand in many areas. Apart from the temporary, uneven, cyclical effects of the recent rise in unemployment, which have struck hard at several professional groups, particularly engineers and scientists, the greatest shortages still tend to be found at high occupational levels, especially in newly emerging fields of specialization.

It is not to be inferred, therefore, that the baccalaureate or professional degree is necessarily the essential passport to employment. On the contrary, it is middle-skilled workers and technicians, not Ph.D.s, that will be most in demand. Indeed, two-thirds of the projected job openings of the seventies will be nonprofessional and nontechnical, arising largely out of replacement needs as older workers retire and as a number of the largest occupational groupings expand. Particularly significant to this study is the continued, expected rapid growth of jobs in the health field, in the human services, and in public service employment of all kinds.

Employment opportunities will abound at technical and semiskilled levels. The acute shortages of professionals in health fields, for example, has already spawned a host of allied paraprofessionals who relieve hard-pressed professionals of some of their tasks as inhalation therapists, X-ray technicians, nurses' aides, laboratory or psychiatric aides. The training of competent technicians and paraprofessionals can be more rapid, requiring less formal education and providing a gateway to occupational mobility for the poor.

Although long-range manpower projections are somewhat unreliable, there is no doubt that all trends point in the same general direction. It is certain that most jobs in the future will require more schooling than in the past, most often in the form of vocational or technical training or apprenticeships. Moreover, with continuing technological advances and changes within the structure of the professions, the lack of a good basic education will preclude participation in new training programs as old skills become obsolete and new opportunities become available. Deficient education may even prevent employment altogether, as surveys in rural and urban poverty areas have already indicated.

In short, for the children born into poverty, a strong back will continue to be less important than a strong education. Education is neither the sole cause nor the single remedy for low productivity and low levels of living, but without literacy, the prospects for achieving self-support are bleak. And without a real command of the three Rs, the possibilities of competing successfully for good jobs and making one's way in a society in which 80% of contemporary youths graduate from high school and nearly 50% go on to higher education are distinctly limited.

To summarize, policies directed toward reducing poverty can be classified into three main categories:

—A full employment and economic growth strategy, which is a fundamental precondition to reducing poverty.
—Income maintenance programs in the form of cash or equivalent goods and services, which are universally needed by the poor.
—A variety of human resources and community development programs aimed at raising the present and future productivity of workers so that they can become self-sufficient.

Institutions of higher education have no direct responsibility or at best a marginal, consultative one, in the first two sets of policy strategems. A major and increasing role can be discerned, however, in human and community development programs in poverty areas. The specific objectives of colleges and universities with regard to the urban poor, however, can only be formulated in terms of the broader goals of the commonwealth, of which they are but one social institution, and in terms of their own special missions, resources and competencies.

Social Policy Goals

The task for society in terms of the urban poor is almost self-evident. It is to fulfill the historic vision of equality of opportunity and promptly translate the ideology into action, into concrete institutionalized behavior.

Two interrelated long-range objectives can be distinguished: (1) to strengthen the channels of upward mobility for the poor and near-poor in educational, occupational and income terms; (2) to assure equality of access for racial, language and ethnic minorities to mainstream social institutions. In the jargon of the social sciences, these are class and caste issues. More simply, the goal is eradicating the vestiges of institutionalized racism and eliminating poverty, hopefully in one generation.

Whether a truly open society and easier social mobility would by itself lead to greater equality, to narrowing the differences between the top and bottom layers in our society, is moot. Whether easier social mobility is indeed possible without first reducing the scale of inequalities and greatly transforming major social institutions is similarly unanswerable. Whether a truly integrated society is attainable in our lifetime is also moot. But in the face of the many obvious bottlenecks to equal opportunity and social mobility and the clear evidence of racial injustices, concern with predicting longe-range outcomes seems somewhat premature.

To put it simply, most people in the United States agree, at least, that a minimum floor of subsistence is needed for all, that the ladders for upward mobility should be truly available to all, and that the serious fissures in the mythical melting pot should be mended. Even this minimum agenda for social action presents a formidable challenge.

The specific challenge with regard to the inhabitants of the urban slum is to find ways to interrupt the cycle of poverty. The objective is to ensure that the hundreds of thousands of children born into poverty, dependency and discrimination are not destined to remain poor.

While most Americans subscribe verbally to this social goal, no such consensus apparently exists in support of even the most obvious means of implementing it, as for example, spending more on the education of a disadvantaged child. To interrupt the cycle of poverty in this generation would require a commitment of public and private resources on a scale commensurate with the problem. It would require an investment in human resources and community development programs of great magnitude and variety. Since deep-seated social change takes time, a sustained commitment over a long period is also necessary.

Furthermore, although the complex of forces converging in the urban slum and perpetuating poverty is readily discernible, the most effective ways of supporting healthy development and reducing the obstacles besetting impoverished families at each stage of the life cycle are not self-evident. In strictly cost-benefit terms, experience has yet to demonstrate which of the proposed cycle-breaking strategies are most effective: investing in early childhood education and day-care centers; inner-city elementary schools; adult manpower training programs; community economic development corporations; supportive social, health and employment services; vocational and technical education for youth; or higher education and professional training for indigenous potential leaders; to name but a few. Each program affects the others.

Housing conditions, transportation and other factors in the physical environment also influence family life and human development significantly. Proposals to improve public transportation, linking inner-city workers with suburban jobs, or those aimed at providing additional housing and employment options for central city workers in the suburbs or in racially integrated new towns or medium-sized cities on principal highway routes are also relevant. New pilot programs and careful evaluation of the effectiveness of existing programs are in order. Higher education is already involved, often peripherally, in many of these activities and can contribute much more directly in the coming decade.

If the effectiveness of alternative poverty strategems is uncertain, it is nevertheless clear that the problems found in the urban slum will not vanish spontaneously, nor will they be washed away in a tide of general affluence. To allow another generation to reach maturity, unskilled, unsocialized and unwanted in a productive, complex society would be to mortgage the future. It would be a profligate waste of human talent, economically as well as morally. Poverty and preventive educational programs are expensive and run counter to the current wave of fiscal retrenchment. But rapid deterioration of the quality of common life, civil disorder beyond our lifetime, and an exponential rise in social costs is the high price of neglect.

4

Roles and Routes for Higher Education

What is the role of higher education with regard to the vast pool of human needs portrayed in the previous chapters? Higher education clearly cannot by itself resolve urban problems, racism, or the interlocking problems of the poor. Nor can it supply needed public services in any significant quantity, even the full range of education services. Other institutions and governmental agencies are specifically charged with responsibility for alleviating poverty and mitigating severe living conditions.

Among the poverty strategems outlined, it is also obvious that all educational institutions have special responsibilities in human resource development, in providing opportunities for self-development. Their role vis-a-vis the poor is primarily cycle-breaking, not care-taking or job-creating.

Education, especially higher education, is an acknowledged avenue of occupational and social mobility, but the role of higher education is more complex. It is both direct and indirect, since it has the capacity to promote long-range, human and community development in a variety of ways. If perceived solely in terms of providing access to higher education to qualified disadvantaged students, its contribution to breaking the cycle of poverty will be exceedingly limited, so relatively small is the proportion of this generation living in abject poverty that can enroll. Statistically, opportunity tends to be seized by the socially advantaged. If conceived exclusively in defensive terms, in building neighborhood programs to smooth troubled town-gown relations, its role is also circumscribed, reactive instead of anticipatory. While both kinds of programs are important now, the multiple role of the public system of higher education flows logically from its several established functions.

Inequalities and Imbalances

Institutions of higher learning regularly engage in a number of activities that can promote community development and extend opportunities for the poor or, contrariwise, fail to do so. What are the functions generally performed by colleges and universities that are potentially significant in breaking the cycle of poverty?

First and most obvious, colleges and universities educate youths and adults, thereby providing avenues for personal achievement and upward mobility for those able to avail themselves of the opportunity. Who will be educated and in what manner are the issues.

43

Second, universities are the chief source of skilled professional manpower across the spectrum of employment. The teachers, health-care workers, urban planners, social workers, and other public servants critical in community development and therefore ultimately in family life and the socialization and education of children, receive their basic education in colleges and universities. Professional education includes more than the mastery of a body of knowledge and intricate techniques. Attitudes, value orientation, and professional ethics are built into the educational process as well. Whether future professionals are attuned and equipped to deal with the poor and render services in poverty areas is in question, as is the very structure of several professions.

Third, university faculties and graduate students undertake research of many kinds, seeking insights and new knowledge in countless ways. Higher education may be a germinal source of ideas and innovations, but it is surely the seat of rigorous analytic techniques and evaluative capabilities potentially applicable to policy questions. The kinds of problems that are addressed and the manner in which research endeavors are conceived and executed are relevant.

Fourth, university faculty consult with and make their professional and technical skills available to public groups in the solution of problems. Which constituencies or publics are served and which neglected is also germane.

Altogether, in the performance of their established functions, institutions of higher education can exert great leverage in removing old roadblocks and building new channels of opportunity for the poor. Altogether, both in what they do and neglect to do, institutions of higher education have a powerful impact on the quality of urban life. Often, these effects are difficult to discern since rarely are they totally exposed and immediately visible. Many public and private institutions impinge more directly and vividly on daily life in the slums, as for example, the systems of justice, health, employment, welfare, housing, transportation and precollegiate education.

Nevertheless, as the chief source of skilled professionals and as a major source of new knowledge and techniques, the influence of higher education on all agencies and institutions operating in the city is pervasive. Because its role is frequently obscure, one step removed in time and space, imbalances in the commitment of resources to narrow constituencies or low-priority, outmoded activities may persist long past the time that they are useful from a contemporary standpoint.

Until recently, the educational and behavioral consequences of past social and economic inequities provided few avenues for spontaneous concourse between slum residents and centers of higher learning. Even when sharing the same living space, traditionally oriented colleges or universities might be, as Clark Kerr has perceptively observed, "in the city but not of the city."

The disjunction between centers of higher learning and the enclaves of poverty lay dormant until relatively recently when the issue of inequality of opportunity rose to new prominence on the national scene. Urbanization, prosperity, and television, together, vividly exposed the disparities in living conditions among different groups in society, quickening latent hopes and aspirations. The rediscovery in the late sixties of intergenerational poverty, underemployment, and hard-core unemployment coincided with the rise of the civil rights movement and has since given educational, manpower, welfare, and community development issues powerful momentum, both off and on the campuses.

It was apparent to black leaders, after 1965, that legal and statutory equality did not necessarily convey equality of access to jobs, housing, health care or higher education, much less equality of results in the near future. While the impetus for social change was organized most vigorously, at first, in black communities, seeds of discontent with persistent poverty and institutionalized inequities took root in many other sectors of society. The issue of social justice, quiescent since the depression, has once again gained prominence in many quarters, including the campuses. It has fueled the "crisis in higher education" and contributed to the "dilemmas of higher education." The "embattled university" has a clear obligation to clarify its stance and review its practices with regard to social justice.

These external pressures coincide with an internal ferment to revitalize teaching and scholarship, to revamp and reform higher education. They also coincide with increasing financial pressures on public institutions, less acute perhaps than those on private colleges but no less restrictive. The issue of social justice has been joined. And conjoined with questions of equity are questions of efficiency and accountability. It is an occasion to be well used.

Reducing Inequalities

At a high level of abstraction, there is almost universal consensus about the chief goal of higher education with regard to the poor. The single transcendent goal, one that state systems are particularly able to fulfill for minorities and impoverished families, is to reduce inequalities of educational opportunity. While equality of opportunity and its corollary, equality of educational opportunity, are ancient ideals, they have yet to be realized in practice. The unfinished business of two hundred years remains on the agenda and conscience of the nation. It is a crucial part of the agenda for public higher education in the seventies.

As to the specific policies and programs that will reduce inequalities, there is much less consensus and much more local variation. A two-pronged approach is advocated in this book, one that roughly corresponds to the earlier analysis of human needs in poverty areas.

The first approach relates to facilitating access to the system itself. This approach has received most attention, bringing significant changes in just the last five years. A review of these changes with an analysis of the formidable barriers that remain and ways to penetrate them is presented in the following three chapters. Since these questions have been much discussed elsewhere, a second set of policy issues are emphasized in the balance of the book, those that relate to improving life chances and living conditions in the poorest areas.

The second approach, operating indirectly through other related social institutions, is geared toward promoting future access to higher education by creating a climate for healthy development and educational achievement in impoverished urban areas. Policy alternatives and guidelines for extending services to the poor are developed in Chapter 8. Other closely related themes concerning education in human service professions, the organization of research and demonstration projects, campus-neighborhood relations, and the intermeshing of metropolitan institutions are explored in the remaining chapters.

Although community service is our subject, services, per se, are but one of the several ways that higher education can help reduce inequalities. In considering the array of functions and services presently performed by state systems in relation to poverty in the urban system, both systems are tangent at a few key points. Six specific spheres of action are immediately apparent, falling within the suggested twofold approach.

First, educational practices and programs can be adapted to better meet the immediate educational needs of talented and motivated individuals from poor communities. Many colleges and universities have already launched small-scale, experimental programs of varying kinds for the "disadvantaged," the effectiveness of which have yet to be evaluated systematically since they are so new. Other students, however, of similar backgrounds and achievement levels are regularly admitted into some public colleges, (particularly the community colleges), and without special help, they quickly drop out. Traditional curricula, methods, and administrative practices are often unsuited to their educational needs, varied learning styles, and tempos. Attrition rates are highest for students from low-income families, particularly black students. A pool of potentially able students of unknown size never even apply for admission. Obstacles, primarily of costs and uneven skills, but also of geography, age, race, family burdens, and improper counseling stand in the way.

Second, a high priority should go to activities designed to improve the overall performance of urban school systems. The public schools in the inner city serve the great mass of students from poor families and often fail to serve them well. There has been a progressive deterioration of measured, educational achievement by students in city schools, segregated by class and race. Although more students of poor families are spending more years in school, the additional years often contribute little to their personal or intellectual development. Passing time in school without much real teaching or learning transpiring is corrosive to the students' personality, to teacher morale, and to the educational system as a whole. Until urban school systems are greatly improved, the opportunities for higher education for low-income and minority students will continue to be short-circuited by deficient early education. Meanwhile, the public colleges which open their doors to the graduates of such schools bear the brunt of earlier failures and the heavy responsibility for offering an authentic chance to learn.

Third and closely related, the quality of vocational and technical education should be greatly improved as a viable alternative to liberal arts education and as its companion. The standard academic curriculum is often unwanted and unsuited to the interests of many youths from low-income families, who then drop out of school with few employable skills. Employment is the chief escape from poverty. Youth unemployment rates in the United States are higher than in any other advanced industrial nation, and the transition from school to work is needlessly difficult. Many of the community colleges and senior colleges are already at work updating and enlarging their curricula offerings. In most high schools, however, less promising students academically are typically shunted into vocational education tracts whose curricula have scarcely passed beyond the manual training and home economics of half a century ago, and an orientation to the working world is virtually absent in conventional elementary schools. If properly taught, the mastery of practical, employable, manipulative skills can stimulate the acquisition of conceptual skills and reinforce self confidence. Institutions of higher education can contribute greatly to the modernization of vocational and technical education, directly, by improving their own community college offerings and, indirectly, by developing new curricula and by training faculty to teach in a variety of settings.

Fourth, the education of professional and technical manpower in human and public service fields can be revised and restructured to meet the needs of inner-city residents. If public schools in poverty areas are woefully deficient in educating their students, similar deficiencies exist in most other public and private services. Progress in improving educational achievement and in fostering the acquisition of advanced skills and disciplines will remain slow without simultaneously improving the total environmental setting of children from poor families. The cycle of poverty tends to reinforce itself, and supportive family and indigenous community institutions are often lacking in neighborhoods where they are most needed. Extended and unrelieved deprivation incubates destructive attitudes, inferior self-images, apathy and alienation, or extreme hostility and aggression, none of which are conducive to education or personal achievement. Local schools are presently the target for hostility in many areas, but it is questionable whether they can be improved without a climate favorable to educational achievement or without simultaneous improvement in other family and community services. Higher education can be a pivotal institution in reforming human service professions.

Fifth, latent skills and interests of concerned faculty and students can be more sharply focused on the resolution of intractable social problems. While many faculty have neither the orientation nor the temperament for social policy questions, others have great capacities and a zest for attacking empirical questions. Faculty research strengths and interests have yet to be organized effectively so as to yield the multiple, interrelated insights required for analyzing complex social problems, for identifying viable policy options, and for evaluating the effectiveness of alternative programs tested in the field. The very subjects of our discussion, breaking the cycle of poverty or educating inner-city children effectively, provide two good examples of complicated, obdurate, social problems. A simple laboratory team "technical" response is inapplicable to "solving" such problems, but many other, alternative modes of eliciting productive responses can be undertaken.

Sixth and last, higher education can facilitate the growth of supportive community institutions essential to healthy development. In neighborhoods where family instability is common and experience circumscribed, the street and television are inordinately influential agents of communication, education, and socialization. Until recently, contemporary urban slums contrasted with those of the early twentieth century in a paucity of indigenous organizations so supportive in the socialization and assimilation of foreign immigrants. The community action program component of the early war on poverty became a focal point for the creation of new community organizations but, to the consternation of public officials, organized frequently around grievances and bent on challenging the power of the establishment. Although the program has been cut back, the social and political forces that were unleashed refuse, like the genie, to go docilely back into the bottle. New community organizations proliferated mostly in black neighborhoods at first, but the style of participatory democracy has since been taken up by many others, by Chicanos, American-Indians, "welfare mothers," "new careerists," and, of course, students. Citizen participation is presently built, as a requirement, into the legislation of a number of federal urban programs, and new community development corporations have been mushrooming in many poverty areas, often enlisting the active cooperation and technical assistance of nearby colleges and universities.

In its relations with newly emergent community leaders and organizations, it is evident that higher education is sailing into unchartered waters, in the eddies of a storm center. When a college happens to be located near an urban slum, its very presence as an institution is significant to its neighbors. Recent experience of colleges suggests that minimal contact and indifference to neighbors more often lead to explosive rather than productive interaction. The forms that new channels of communication and cooperation might take and the adaptation of traditional extension and community development services to the contemporary urban scene are highlighted in the last chapters.

Higher Education in Perspective

If higher education is vulnerable to indictment for perpetrating social inequities, it is less on grounds of malfeasance than of nonfeasance. More simply, it is less a question of committing discriminatory and exclusionary acts deliberately than of failing to act appropriately or to perceive clearly the full extent of its responsibilities. Individual institutions and faculty have been actively engaged in each of the activities outlined in the previous section. They are familiar ones since they fall squarely within the traditional missions of particular colleges or universities. But because they are often isolated, uncoordinated efforts of small scale and uneven quality in both conception and execution, their effectiveness varies widely.

Although there is a long way to go towards meeting educational needs in the inner city, progressive changes were undertaken in many states during the sixties towards open, urban, systems and toward reducing geographic and rural imbalances; the framework for further progress has been erected. State systems have been most alert and most successful thus far in greatly expanding the opportunities for working-class students to go to college and in absorbing the flood of youths reaching college age in the late sixties. They have typically been less alert to the full pedagogical implications of rapid growth, to the internal adaptations needed to educate new kinds of students coming from a wider spectrum of society, and to their other potential responsibilities towards the poor.

Higher education in the United States, viewed in its totality, might appear relatively open, diverse, and egalitarian compared with many European systems. In 1970, almost half of the college-age population in the nation sought out some sort of education beyond high school, which is twice the proportion in any other nation and eight to ten times that of most advanced, industrial countries.[a] The college-going rate in the United States has increased tenfold since the turn of the century. Furthermore, the educational destinies of children are not fixed at puberty in the United States as in many European nations with bifurcated elementary and high-school curricula which determine at an early age occupation and social class. In theory, opportunities for many kinds of higher education are open to any who can benefit, including late bloomers and adults.

The community colleges, in conception, are the most egalitarian and open institutions of any, and they comprise an increasingly large sector within higher education. For the urban poor, they are pivotal institutions, but their precise role in the coming decade has yet to emerge with clarity. Will they mostly attempt to replicate the first two years of the traditional liberal arts curricula? Will they evolve into technical training institutions serving all ages? Will they become effective, unique vehicles for innovative educational and service programs for the poor? Or will they successfully combine all three major roles with other cultural and community ones in proportions that will vary locally, as presently conceived?

The curriculum offerings, even in the graduate faculties of state universities, are also extraordinarily diverse and egalitarian, bearing little resemblance to the classical trivium and quadrivium. Advanced degrees are offered in a wide range of fields, from such seemingly abstract subjects as analytic philosophy or structural linguistics to such eminently worldly and practical pursuits as park adminis-

---

[a]Growth and changes in college enrollments are more fully reviewed in Chapter 5.

tration, rehabilitation services, dairy technology, sanitary engineering, criminology, or health education.

Despite the seeming openness of the educational system, the comprehensive and egalitarian curricula of state colleges, the destinies of many children tend to be fixed, nonetheless effectively, by the social class of their families. The process is more subtle perhaps than in European countries. The whole continuum of education acts as a social sieve so that the stratification in the social system can be discerned in the stratification within state systems of higher education. The kinds of obstacles encountered by upwardly aspiring students in state colleges are various, including marked differences in the quality of instruction, inadequate information about entrance requirements or financial aids, lack of articulation within the system, and others. To reduce inequalities these kinds of roadblocks to mobility and achievement must be identified and promptly removed.

With regard to extension and continuing education, a relatively small proportion of the total resources devoted to these activities reach the urban poor. The historical roots of many state systems reveal themselves in the heavy weighting of rural as against urban extension programs, especially at universities that evolved from land-grant colleges. Even today, for example, when the farm population of Illinois is near 5% of the state total, almost half of the formal extension budget of the University of Illinois is devoted to its agricultural, cooperative extension. In 1966-67, of the total expenditures for extension amounting to $14.1 million, $6.6 million were allocated to cooperative extension.[b] To be sure, a great many of the major public service activities of the University of Illinois are not subsumed under the "extension" budget, and the cooperative extension itself is in transition, increasingly shifting its services toward urban groups. Nevertheless, relative proportions in rural vs. urban programs appear out of balance in many states, whether viewed on a per capita or problem basis.

The success of cooperative extension and agricultural experiment stations in raising farm productivity and improving living conditions in rural areas inspires confidence that "urban extension" programs and "urban grant" colleges might similarly succeed. While a number of features distinguishing the client-oriented, informal, practical emphasis of cooperative extension can be transposed to an urban slum, others cannot. Most of all, the reciprocal flow of support for higher education from a grateful constituency, expressed through its elected representatives in the legislature, the natural quid pro quo, cannot be expected in an urban setting. The heterogeneity of the city, racial tensions, and the fragmentation of governmental authority and private decision-making virtually guarantee conflicts of interests in the determination of social goals and public policies.

---

[b]The extension budget for 1967-68, was divided as follows.[1]

Division of University Extension	$ 3,224,563
Cooperative Extension (1966-7)	6,620,446
Division of Services for Crippled Children (Medical Center Campus)	4,302,819
	$14,147,828

While much can be learned from the long history of successes and failures of agricultural extension programs that is applicable to "urban extension" or "urban grant" colleges, two aspects of the analogy are most apt. First, the inter-disciplinary, problem-oriented, client-centered approach that has characterized agricultural extension has worked well in rural areas, and even though the component elements would be different in cities, the approach might also bring positive changes. Second, the sustained public commitment, expressed over the course of a century in the allocation of federal and state revenues to improve rural life is what is sorely needed in urban programs to improve urban life. Effective urban poverty programs are no less costly than rural ones, and little more than small-scale, prototypical programs can be undertaken by higher education without major increases in appropriations for urban service programs.

In sum, improving the performance in functions traditionally ascribed to higher education and redirecting these functions to serve the needs of the cities and of the poor remain unfinished. The gulf between verbalized objectives and institutionalized behavior can be closed over the course of the seventies. To illustrate specific ways to close the gap and translate abstract goals into concrete programs, the system of higher education in a single state, Illinois, will be used as a case study. The Illinois public system is prototypical in conception, if not in performance, of an open, egalitarian, pluralistic model.

Part Two:

5 Widening Opportunities

Higher education in the United States has undergone profound changes over the course of the century, but none more dramatic than its rapid expansion in the last decade. The increase solely in the sheer number of students enrolled in colleges during the sixties represents the most sustained and rapid growth in the entire universal history of higher education. Its very growth poses a series of new questions for the poor, since equality of access to higher education is still a distant prospect. Before addressing the specific remaining impediments and the unresolved policy questions left in the wake of rapid expansion, an overview of past and probable future aggregate changes in higher education is needed.

Another, closely related, set of questions concern the nature and quality of the education offered in post-high school institutions since access alone is a spurious goal if educational programs are unsuited to the needs of prospective students. Some of these questions are discussed in later chapters where learning and service programs are melded together. A third, related set of questions revolve around the complex issue of equity, around public policies tending mostly to subsidize the education of endowed and accomplished youths while slighting others. Since these are intricate questions, much discussed elsewhere, they will not be pursued deeply here.[1] This chapter and the following two focus chiefly on the inequalities still prevailing in access to college itself and the avowed or tacit commitment of public colleges and universities to eliminate them.

Within this restricted context, it is evident that despite recent rapid expansion, higher education as presently constituted is not a possibility for many able minority youths or for a larger, less obviously absent pool of white youths. Nor are there many institutionalized alternative channels of opportunity and training open to the poor in youth or later years. A social vacuum exists, and a number of urban community colleges have been attempting to fill the void by offering new avenues for development and achievement. How far community colleges and other colleges and universities have already progressed toward providing educational opportunities for the poor will be reviewed in order to ascertain the way that each has yet to go.

Rapid Expansion in Higher Education

College-going rates have been rising steadily in the United States for decades, but they shot up dramatically during the last decade. College enrollments in 1970 were more than double those in only 1960. About 7.6 million students in 1970, or almost half of all college-age youths in the nation, attended college or post-high school institutions. The 3.5 million college students in 1960, in turn, was double their number in 1940, when about 1.6 million students were enrolled.[2]

By 1970, of all high school graduates between 20 and 24 years old, 52.4% of the young men and 41.7% of the young women, had completed at least one year of college. The comparable percentages in 1960 were 42.2% among men and 32.8% among women. In addition, 16.4% of all young adults between 25 and 29 had completed at least four years of college, while the comparable proportion in their parents' generation in 1940 was only 5.8%.[3]

The extraordinary expansion in higher education in the last ten years, with the attendant growth in facilities, faculties, personnel and expenditures, represented more than an accommodation to the flood of postwar babies who reached maturity in the late sixties. It reflected as well a genuine effort to provide access to higher education to a wider sector of society than in the past. About two-fifths of the 1960-70 increase in college enrollments was attributable to an increase in the number of persons of college-going age, while three-fifths could be ascribed to an increase in the proportion of youths seeking higher education. The percentage of black youths in college rose most rapidly, surpassing average rates of growth, but racial differentials in college attendance nevertheless persisted (see Table 5-1).

The sharp rise in enrollments, in effect, has meant that two out of three college students in 1970 came from families whose parents had not attended college themselves. It has been suggested that this educational gap, with its attitudinal and social concomitants, is a significant part of the alleged generation gap.[4] And perhaps the sometime dysjunction in the aims and values of faculty and those of their students may be partially ascribed to this same source. Among white college students in 1969, 61% were from families whose head had not attended college, including 24% without even a high school degree. Among black college students, the comparable educational gap was greater, with 71% from families whose head had not gone to college and 50% who had not completed high school (see Table 5-2).

Table 5-1
United States College Enrollments by Race, October 1969 and 1964*

Race	Enrolled, 1969		Enrolled, 1964	
	Number	Percent	Number	Percent
All races	7,435	100.0	4,643	100.0
White	6,827	91.8	4,337	93.4
Black	492	6.6	234	5.0
Other	116	1.6	72	1.6

*Persons 16-34 years old, in thousands, civilian noninstitutional population.
Source: U.S. Bureau of the Census.

Table 5-2
United States Educational Attainment by Race, 1940-1970*

Year and Race	Percent by Level of School Completed	
	4 Years of High School or More	4 Years of College or More
All races:		
1970	75.4	16.4
1969	74.7	16.0
1968	73.2	14.7
1967	72.5	14.6
1964	69.2	12.8
1960	60.7	11.1
1950	51.7	7.7
1940	37.8	5.8
White:		
1970	77.8	17.3
1969	77.0	17.0
1968	75.3	15.6
1967	74.8	15.5
1964	72.1	13.6
1960	63.7	11.8
1950	55.2	8.1
1940	41.2	6.4
Black and other races:		
1970	58.4	10.0
1969	57.5	9.1
1968	57.6	7.9
1967	55.7	8.3
1964	48.0	7.0
1960	38.6	5.4
1950	23.4	2.8
1940	12.1	1.6

Level of school completed by persons 25 to 29 years old.
Source: U.S. Bureau of the Census.

Turning these figures around in the case of black college students, one finds that 29% of their parents had gone to college, and half were high school graduates. In the light of the fierce discrimination and the wider racial differentials in education prevailing in their parents' youth, it appears probable that colleges may have merely creamed the more advantaged, upperstrata among blacks for most of their present students without, as yet, reaching very deeply into ordinary working-class families.

The public sector of higher education has been its principal growth sector so that, by 1970, about 70% of all college students were enrolled in public institutions of higher learning. Although public institutions comprise little more than a third of the entire group of roughly 2,400 separate institutions of higher education in the United States, they tend to be much larger than private ones.

In some states, public systems are of an astounding size and complexity. For example, the State University in New York enrolled 320,000 students on 72 campuses in 1971, and City University of New York had an additional 200,000 students on 20 campuses. The 9 campuses of the University of California enrolled 106,000 students in 1969 while the California State College System with 19 campuses had 242,000 students. The California community college system is still more vast and complex, the most fully developed of any state. In fact, the California three-tier system of the community college, the state college, and the university, with corresponding ascending levels of selectivity in admissions and distance from home, has become the model for a number of other state plans.

The most conspicuous recent development in higher education has been the spectacular growth of community colleges. Within the public sector, it is the two-year, open-door, low-cost, comprehensive community college that is its growth sector. This distinctively, but not exclusively, American invention traces its origins to the junior colleges and technical institutes founded earlier in the century, but not until the fifties did the comprehensive, public community colleges really begin to proliferate.

Enrollments in two-year colleges have been growing at more than twice the rate of all other institutions of higher education (see Table 5-3). By 1960, about 600,000 students were enrolled in over 600 two-year colleges, and by 1970, about 2,000,000 students, both part-time and full-time, were in attendance at over a thousand institutions. Approximately 50 new community colleges have opened their doors each year since the mid-sixties, roughly one each week.[5] But growth has been very uneven in different parts of the country. One-third of all community colleges in 1968 were to be found in only 7 states (California, Florida, Illinois, Michigan, New York, Texas and Washington), which together accounted for more than two-thirds of student enrollments.[6]

Table 5-3
Degree-Credit Enrollments in Two-Year Colleges, 1958-1968

	(In thousands)		
Enrollment	1958	1968	Percent Change
Total enrollments	3,236	6,758	108.8
Junior colleges	386	1,164	201.6
Other higher education	2,851	5,595	96.2

Source: U.S. Bureau of Labor Statistics.

The open-access, urban community college has been the greatest single force, thus far, for extending new opportunities for higher education to underrepresented minorities and impecunious city dwellers. The proximity of low-cost, flexible, commuter institutions has been a pivotal factor in college entrance for thousands of students with limited resources, some of whom must contribute to their family support.[a] Yet, viewing the whole array, the performance of individual colleges has been exceedingly variable with regard to acknowledging and discharging educational responsibilities toward minorities and the poor.

The strains of rapid growth are apparent. The assimilation of community colleges into state systems and their articulation with senior institutions is still ragged at a number of junctures. Many community colleges are going through an identity crisis as to their missions and methods. They have been cast in the role of the people's college to perform for contemporary urban society a new role somewhat comparable to that of the land-grant college or the comprehensive high school early in the century. In several state plans, they are the chosen instrument for extending new educational services to community areas, rural and suburban as well as inner city. Consequently, the devolution of their programs and policies is a question of considerable importance. One such state is Illinois, to which we now turn for a closer look at the specific impact of broad national trends.

Growth of Illinois Public System

During the fifties, the majority of students in Illinois attended private colleges or universities. By 1961, enrollments in public institutions surpassed those in private ones, and the balance has continued to shift since then, as increasing numbers of students of working-class families entered lower cost public colleges.[8]

The number of students enrolled in post-high school educational institutions, both public and private, in Illinois more than doubled during the sixties, as in the nation. Much of the increase in enrollment was accommodated through a planned expansion of the public system of higher education. Growth of the latter was extraordinarily rapid, with enrollments soaring from 96,000 students in 1960 to 325,000 students in Fall 1970, an increase of some 338%. A network of commuter and community colleges in populous areas of the state was established and enlarged after 1965; it is still under construction.

Of the 138 institutions of higher education in Illinois in 1969, the 44 public institutions enrolled 63% of all undergraduates. Largely because of the proliferation of public community colleges throughout the state, three-fourths of all freshmen and sophomores were enrolled in public institutions. A similar, delayed shift has been occurring more recently in upper division and graduate school en-

[a]Trent and Medsker's research indicates that if a college is within commuting distance, half of all high school graduates will attend, while if there is none nearby, only one-third of the class will go to college.[7]

rollments as well. By 1969, public institutions enrolled 51.2% of students in junior and senior levels, 56.4% in master's degree programs, and 64.9% in doctoral degree programs. Among the professional schools in Illinois, such as health institutions, law schools, or fine arts conservatories, however, private institutions predominate, absorbing a declining, but nevertheless major, proportion of all enrollments. In 1969, they accounted for more than three-fourths of the total. Increasing pressure for admissions to low-cost graduate and professional schools in the Chicago area can be anticipated as the ranks of penurious college graduates begin to swell.

Looking ahead, it would appear that further expansion of public colleges and universities, particularly urban institutions, is required to meet the anticipated demand for undergraduate admissions in the seventies. Private colleges and universities in Illinois, as in every state, are exceedingly diverse, both in purpose and social composition, with the largest and most prestigious drawing a major proportion of their students from other states. Several in Chicago, such as Roosevelt University or Central YMCA College, have been in the vanguard of innovative institutions serving minority and low-income students. Others, in less populous regions, have been the chief sources of whatever educational, cultural, or developmental public services are available in their regions. Most of them, however, are under tight financial strictures at the present time and do not generally conceive of their public responsibilities on any scale commensurate with existing educational needs. The levers therefore for extending opportunity are vested primarily in the public domain.

Anticipating Future Demand

Looking toward the next decade, pressures for admission to college will undoubtedly increase, making for difficult choices in the precise timing and allocation of the narrowing stream of resources for higher education. Any plans for expanding opportunities and improving higher education in the coming decade must take account of several competing factors.

—The size of the college-age population will increase until 1980, and the proportion of the population seeking postsecondary education will also rise.
—The pressure on enrollment will be most acute in major cities, where at least two-thirds of the college-age population resides, as do the preponderant number of minority and middle- or low-income, potential students.
—Students on campus will reflect a wider sector of the social spectrum with correspondingly diversified aims, ages, learning styles, and educational needs.
—An increasing number of youths graduating from deficient and segregated high schools, will seek and gain admission to state colleges, ill-prepared for higher education.

—The community college is both a promising and a portentous solution to the mounting pressures for broader educational opportunities, (promising of economy, diversity and local responsiveness; portentous of stratification and de facto segregation within higher education comparable to that now found in lower schools).

These conclusions are derived from observing the implication of current changes in higher education. If tuitions and other costs to students continue to rise faster than available financial aids, however, higher education will be beyond the reach of many aspiring poor and working-class potential students.

The confluence of a number of trends accounted for the rapidly increased enrollments of the sixties, most of which can be expected to prevail in the coming decade. Two major factors can be identified: 1) an increase in the number of youths of college age; and 2) a rise in the propensity to attend college.

As for the first, the college-age population in the nation will continue to grow during the seventies, but at a gradually decelerating rate, reaching a peak in 1980. The growth curve then turns downward to bottom out near current levels after 1986.[b] Although the rate of growth will decelerate, the increment in the actual number of youths reaching college age in the seventies is nearly the same as in the sixties.[c] Furthermore, a higher proportion in the pool of potential students will be black or Hispanic-Americans, reflecting earlier, higher birth rates. A greater proportion will also reside in large metropolitan areas. Altogether, if costs of construction, operations and personnel continue to rise as in the past, it seems certain the public systems will find themselves running hard just to stay in the same place by 1980.

The second major trend likely to continue into the seventies is the increase in the proportion of the total population seeking post-high school education. The college-going rate (defined as the number of degree-credit students of any age enrolled per each 100 persons of college age), for example, rose in Illinois from 41.7% in 1960 to an estimated 64% in 1970. The propensity to attend college varies widely among states and mirrors, with little distortion, actual differences in local opportunities. The proportion of Illinois residents attending college, for example, is higher than national averages, almost comparable to the college-going

[b]Barring unforeseen catastrophes, projections in the number of youths reaching college age are reliable until 1988 since prospective students are already born.[9] In Illinois, the corresponding rate of increase in the college-age cohort of about 24% is estimated between 1970 and 1980 as compared with the 46% increase between 1960 and 1970. The increment in Illinois amounts to nearly 200,000 students.

[c]According to an independent set of projections by the Carnegie Commission, total college enrollment in the nation will increase by 59% between 1970 and 1980, compared with an increase of 124% actual between 1960 and 1970, but the increment in the actual number of college students by 1980 will amount to between four and five million persons, a number comparable to the increment during the sixties.[10]

rate in New York, but considerably lower than the estimated 75% rate in California.

Without any special efforts to recruit minorities or students of limited means, the proportion of both young and adult persons seeking admission to institutions of higher education will surely increase during the seventies. The main reasons for the certain upward trend in college-going can be identified, even though precise quantitative enrollment projections are somewhat more hazardous.

First, education tends to create its own demand for further education, and with rising educational levels throughout the nation, more students will be completing high school. High school attendance has become almost universal in the United States, with 94% of the age group presently in attendance and about 80% graduating.[10] In a sense, the vast majority of the generation of young people now coming to maturity are candidates for higher education, either in the next few years or over the course of their lives.[d]

Second, the economic prosperity of the late sixties permitted more parents to send their children to college or to enroll themselves. There is every prospect that, apart from temporary, cyclical downswings, overall standards of living will continue to rise so that spending more years in school becomes increasingly feasible economically. While the postindustrial, cybernetic era of leisure is not on the immediate horizon, the trends toward late entry into the labor force and early retirement will undoubtedly continue. Furthermore, the burgeoning of knowledge in professional fields and technological advances in industry will give added impetus to the adult education essential in the renewal of old skills and the acquisition of new ones.

Third, the participation of females in the labor force, especially of mature, married women, has risen significantly. Increased future demands for higher education by both young and adult women can be anticipated. Women comprised 37% of the total labor force in 1968.[11] Over 42% of all women of working age were gainfully employed, with half of the employed women older than 40 years of age. Employment, however, was concentrated in lower occupational levels and heavily weighted towards traditionally female occupations, such as clerical workers, health and human service workers, and lower-school teachers, already in oversupply. The median income of full-time, year-round female workers, many of whom are the chief breadwinners in the family, was only $4,560 compared with a median income of $7,814 for male workers. The differential in pay scales, by sex, for comparable jobs, narrows as one ascends the occupational hierarchy. Although college attendance has been rising, women in 1967 received only 40% of all bachelor's degrees, 34.7% of master's degrees, and 11.9% of the doctorates granted. A growing demand from women for part-time and full-time

---

[d]College attendance among older students has been rising. For example, the percentage of college students 25 to 35 years of age tripled between 1950 and 1970 (see *New Students and New Places*).

adult education can be expected as pressure mounts to eliminate sexual discrimination in education and employment.

Fourth, aspirations are also rising, especially among young people from working-class and minority group families. More children with limited financial backing will surely seek the advanced education and training denied their parents. Between 1939 and 1959, the increase in college attendance from all income groups was roughly uniform, but between 1960 and 1966, a new trend began to emerge as proportionately more young people from working-class and low-income families entered colleges.[12] The high percentages of recent graduates of Chicago's public high schools hoping to go to college, even from the lowest achieving schools, are presented in Table 2-5 as an example. How many such students will actually realize their ambition, enter colleges and successfully complete their degrees will be determined largely by state educational policies and the resources provided for community and senior colleges.

Policy Implications

Before turning to that question, two policy implications for future planning are to be emphasized. First, projections of rapidly growing, future college enrollments are very likely to be in error if they are mechanical, straightline projections from the past. A point will be reached where one can profitably go no further in admitting students of low educational achievement without substantially improving preschools and elementary schools.[13] Second, before that point is approached, the composition of collegiate student bodies, in terms of social class, race-ethnicity, age, experience and personal objectives, will be far more heterogeneous than in any past time.

A host of unresolved educational issues flow from the undoubtedly increasing social heterogeneity of future college students. Ironically, while higher education has grown rapidly, greatly enlarging the scale of opportunity, it has not grown more diverse. In fact, it has tended to become more stratified and standardized.[14] The public sector, as we have seen, has borne the brunt of expansion in serving mounting waves of new students. This has been accomplished, in many places, by increasing the number of students registered in existing public institutions rather than by increasing the number and variety of institutions themselves.[15] As a result, both state systems and public institutions are often of a massive size.

The maintenance of diversity in structure and function among separate autonomous institutions within a state system therefore becomes all the more essential. While standards of educational achievement and of excellence can be uniform, the means of attaining them can and should be subject to great variation among and within institutions, thereby providing more educational options most economically.

In particular, the question is posed as to whether urban community colleges or senior commuter colleges will succeed in devising new, more effective ways of reaching and teaching low-achieving, low-income students. Will they be able at the same time to offer open routes to the highest reaches of professional and academic achievement?

The question is also posed as to whether huge institutions are desirable for educating a student body with increasingly heterogeneous backgrounds and aims. Revised pedagogical techniques and course material; flexible schedules and calendars; a plurality of curricula offerings; regrouping into smaller, collegiate clusters; in sum, new approaches to teaching and learning of the kind suggested in many other specialized studies are clearly required.[16] Without internal adaptations to teach new kinds of students, expansion can swamp effective education in the colleges, as it already has in many urban high schools. In short, significant enrollment increases should be closely synchronized with internal academic reform.

6 Sources of Inequality

The barriers to higher education are multiple, complex and reinforcing, including barriers of distance, age, family problems, inadequate information, and others, but the chief sources of inequality coalesce around a relatively few factors. The probability of attending college declines sharply if one's parents are poor or dark-skinned, or both. College attendance is directly related to family income and educational level. The Census Bureau tells us that "among families with dependents of college-age in 1969, 66% of the families with incomes of $15,000 or more had a dependent member attending college full-time as compared to only 16% of the families with incomes under $3,000."[1] Blacks are comparatively underrepresented in colleges since poverty, discrimination and deficient early schooling conjoin for more than a third of all black families. While solid statistics are scarce, each of the latter factors will be examined, in turn, in order to assess its effect on college attendance.

Segregation

Until Fall 1965, when the federal government deliberately counted students by color, information about college attendance by race was very sketchy. Even today, after several major surveys, the racial data that have become available remain quite unreliable, full of inconsistencies, useful only for crude comparisons, with blacks as the only minority group in college of a size sufficient to warrant close statistical analysis.

The virtual absence on all but a few campuses of Hispanic-American students, relative to their numbers in the nation, is striking. Americans, whose native language is Spanish and who are usually counted as white, comprised 5% of the nation's population in 1970, in toto, about 9.2 million persons, but college enrollments were statistically insignificant in all but a few places.[a] Aspira, an agency that provides guidance and financial aid to Puerto Rican high school and college students, for example, had assisted only 1,958 college students altogether by 1969, four years after it began operations nationally. Yet, there are about 1.45 million Puerto Ricans living in the United States. Apart from the problems Hispanic-Americans share with other minority groups, the language barrier is par-

---

[a]Of the 9.2 million persons whose native language is Spanish, the largest subgroup was Mexican-American (55%); the second largest was Puerto Rican (15.8%); the third largest was Cuban (6.1%); and the balance trace their origins to a variety of other countries. Of the total, 80% were native-born citizens of the nation while the remaining 20% comprise the single, largest, foreign-born group in the United States.[2]

ticularly formidable in education because language is a principal cognitive tool. In a sense, Hispanic-American children start dropping out on the first day of kindergarten.[b]

As for American Indians, less than half of the reservation Indians complete high school while the dropout rate from urban high schools is unknown but estimated to be even higher.[3] In contrast, students from Japanese-American or Chinese-American families are relatively well-represented in college, indeed over-represented statistically in graduate and professional schools. Orientals, therefore, are omitted from our subsequent discussion of minority enrollments even though they do confront discrimination in some quarters, as do Jewish students and several other religious and immigrant minorities.

Blacks, of course, compose the largest single racial minority in the nation, particularly in the nation's largest cities. In 1964, it was found that 4.6% of all college students were black as compared with the 11.5% black college-age youths in the population.[4] Over half attended all-black colleges in the South, leaving only upwards of 2% of the remaining black college students dispersed throughout the country among racially integrated colleges and universities. Relatively few were enrolled in universities or graduate schools, the highest proportion attending state colleges with low tuitions and high dropout rates. Approximately 30% were freshmen.[c]

Since then, college attendance by black students has risen sharply and changed significantly in its distribution. Nevertheless, the differentials in college-going rates between black and white students remain wide (see Table 5-1). The Census Bureau reported that in 1969, black students comprised approximately 6.6% of all United States college students, totaling 492,000 persons. The increase between 1964 and 1969 was very rapid, amounting to 258,000 persons or 110% in only five years. This was a rate of increase more than twice as fast as the growth of total college enrollments during the period.[d] In only one year, between Fall 1968 and 1969, enrollments in midwest colleges were estimated to have advanced by about 25%.[5]

A different, noncomparable set of data from the Bureau of Labor Statistics, confirms the rapid rise in college entrance among nonwhites. In 1963, 38% of nonwhite, high school graduates entered college, and by 1968, this rate had risen

---

[b]Knowledgeable persons in the Chicago public school system, for example, estimate that 70% of Spanish-speaking students do not complete high school.

[c]Black enrollments in Illinois colleges generally conformed to the national pattern, probably amounting to 2-3% of the total, but heavily concentrated at lower division levels and in a relatively few institutions.

[d]John Egerton in *Change* (Summer 1970), questions the validity of the Census Bureau estimates, based on a survey of households. He argues that they overstate black enrollments by one to two per cent when compared with the fragmentary data spliced together from campus surveys.

to 46%, while the rate of college entrance among white students was about 57%.[6]

Blacks presently comprise about 12% of the college-age population in the United States but represent a much higher proportion of the children of the nation, for example, about 16% of all elementary school students, which reflects earlier, high birth rates and a younger age distribution. Looking toward the future, the number of black students attending college would have to rise at an even more rapid rate in the seventies than in the late sixties in order to narrow racial differentials in education achievement.

A major shift also occurred during the sixties in where black students went to college, a shift laden with policy implications. Of all black college students in 1970, it is estimated that approximately one-third (34%) attended historic black colleges; another third (32%) were enrolled in public two-year institutions; another fourth (26%) were dispersed among public senior institutions, leaving less than 8% in attendance at other kinds of institutions.[7]

Scarcely five years before, you will recall that more than half of the nation's black students were enrolled in traditionally all-black colleges, largely in southern states. In fact, looking back ten years to 1960, two-thirds of the nation's black students attended historic all-black colleges. The single factor, most salient to increasing college attendance by black students, has been the recent accessibility, economically, geographically and academically, of urban commuter colleges. Even though approximately the same number of students were enrolled in historic black colleges as in public community colleges, the latter attracted almost half of all new black freshmen in 1970.[8] Once again, the community college emerges as a strategic institution, invested with heavy responsibilities for educating nonwhite students.

In Illinois, as in other populous industrial states, the propensity of black students to attend a relatively few urban public institutions is even more pronounced and worth a closer look since somewhat more specific information is available.[e] In 1970, nearly one-third (32.7%) of all black college students enrolled in the 130-odd institutions of higher learning in Illinois attended a single

[e]Under the auspices of the U.S. Department of Health, Education and Welfare, Civil Rights Division, a racial survey was undertaken of students enrolled, Fall 1970, in every college in the nation receiving federal funds. The preliminary Illinois tabulations from this survey were made available to the writer in advance of publication and are the sources of Tables 6-1, 6-3, 6-4, 6-5 and 6-6, and of the percentages cited in the text. In field visits to colleges in Illinois, additional information was collected, for example, Table 6-2. Some of the discrepancies in enrollment figures arise from differing ways of counting part-time, nonmatriculated students. The latter factor is the source of the seeming discrepancies between Tables 6-2 and 6-3. In any case, the comparability of racial data is suspect, except for broad comparisons, since estimating methods vary in each institution. Enrollment figures by race in the Circle Campus of the University of Illinois, located in Chicago, were not available since student enrollments on all three campuses of the University of Illinois were aggregated together. Over 1,000 black students were probably registered at the Circle Campus, as well as a small but significant number of students of other races, near 500 persons, out of a total student body of over 15,000 persons.

institution, the City Colleges of Chicago (see Tables 6-1 and 6-2). The latter is a public, comprehensive, community college network, with seven campuses located in different neighborhoods of the central city. In fact, among the more comparable number of black freshmen and sophomores in any Illinois college, an even higher proportion (42.8%) were students at the City Colleges of Chicago. To see how this comes about, an enlarged, statewide, frame-of-reference is needed.

A survey by the U.S. Department of Health, Education and Welfare revealed that by 1970, more than 8% of the students at all Illinois colleges, public or private, at any grade level, were black, and an additional 2% were of other minority groups (Table 6-3). As a point of reference, the nonwhite population in Illinois, altogether in 1970, amounted to 13.6% of the state's total (see Table B-5). Quite clearly, and quite recently as well, the graduates of high schools in the poverty areas and segregated neighborhoods of Chicago, East St. Louis and other cities have increasingly found their way into college. Black students, for example, comprised only about 5.6% of all freshmen in Illinois colleges in 1967, with the proportion of women students amounting to 6.9%, noticeably higher than that of men at 4.4%. Since then, the percentages have risen rapidly in Illinois, as they have elsewhere, with blacks composing some 11.4% of all freshmen in the state's colleges in 1970.[f]

This increase in minority student enrollment can largely be ascribed to the planned expansion of the Illinois public system after 1966, which emphasized the creation of low-cost commuter institutions, in particular, a network of community colleges, ultimately to blanket every region of the state and several new urban senior institutions. The community colleges were expressly charged in the state plan with the responsibility for admitting all comers, offering remedial courses to sharpen skills of otherwise able and motivated students, and providing a comprehensive variety of educational options, including transfer programs that parallel the first two years offered in senior colleges, and terminal employment-oriented programs. A few, accordingly, have been doing yeoman duty for inner-city blacks, isolated rural students, mature men and women, and others with special educational needs.

Approximately 1.3 million blacks live in the Chicago area, about 86.3% of those in the state (see Table B-2). It is therefore not surprising that black enrollments in the City Colleges of Chicago far exceed those found anywhere else in Illinois. In October 1968, for example, the City Colleges of Chicago estimated that black students comprised 33% of all enrollments, amounting to over 11,000 persons, which proportion accurately mirrored the ratio of blacks to whites residing in the city (32.6%). The proportion of black students attending the City Colleges of Chicago has continued to rise and by October 1970, amounted to 40.4% of total enrollments or 12,697 students. Adding together the number of

---

[f]The comparable proportion of black freshmen in the nation's colleges was 8.3% in 1970 according to preliminary estimates of HEW.

students of all minority groups, one finds that white students comprised about half of total enrollments (54.5%) in 1970, a considerably lower proportion than in the citywide population.

Nor is it surprising that enrollments on each of its seven Chicago campuses varied according to race and tended to reflect segregated, residential patterns and segregated, high school district patterns. Two of the campuses, Malcolm X and Kennedy-King, were virtually all black, while Wright, Southwest and Amundsen-Mayfair enrolled quite low percentages of minority students, and enrollments in the remaining colleges ranged between the two poles, with blacks only recently picking up a slight majority.

The contrast with nearby public community colleges in the suburban ring of Chicago is vivid (see Table 6-4). Only a tiny core of nonwhite students gained entrance to the 13 suburban community colleges, and all but three colleges enrolled less than one hundred nonwhite students. So long as community colleges in metropolitan areas are organized and partially financed by local, geographically based districts and so long as residential segregation also prevails in cities, de facto segregation is an inevitable outcome in presumably open-door colleges.

Even when the options reside solely with the student, which is not the case in two-year colleges, proximity, with the accompanying economies in transportation costs and student time, also plays a part in college choice for hard-pressed, minority students who are poor. The marked differences in the racial composition of the student bodies in two sister public senior colleges in Chicago, each with virtually identical missions and size and each located at opposite ends of the city, portray this graphically (Tables 6-5 and 6-6). At Chicago State College on the southwest side of the city, 6 out of 10 students were nonwhite; at Northeastern Illinois State College on the northwest side of the city, only 1 in 10 were nonwhite. These differences reflect, quite tangibly, the racial and socioeconomic imbalances that prevail among residential districts in every large city.

East St. Louis contains the second largest concentration of black families in Illinois, amounting to 5% of the state total. A new community college was recently established there expressly to serve an economically depressed, segregated district, and it is exceptional in that it is totally state-funded, requiring no matching local contribution. Several other community colleges near the miniature ghettos throughout the state also admit significant proportions of black students even though, in absolute numbers, enrollment totals are small.

Among senior colleges and universities, most of the well-established ones have been actively recruiting minority and "educationally disadvantaged" students into new experimental, educational programs. Mostly small in scale, they were presumably designed to point the way to effective, larger-scale programs. Although precise, statewide, enrollment counts and differential costs are not available, these "special educational opportunity programs," in the colleges visited by the writer included only a tiny fraction of students at freshmen and perhaps sophomore levels and appeared to be very expensive on a per capita basis. Cri-

Table 6-1

Enrollments in the City Colleges of Chicago by Race, October 1970, All Campuses (Full-Time Equivalent)*

All Campuses	Total All Races	White Number	White Percent	Black Number	Black Percent	Spanish-American Number	Spanish-American Percent	American-Indian Number	American-Indian Percent	Oriental-American Number	Oriental-American Percent
Undergraduate	16,482	7,770	47.1	7,987	48.5	464	2.8	44	.3	217	1.3
First Year	10,968	4,969	45.3	5,535	50.5	309	2.8	24	.2	131	1.2
Second Year	5,514	2,801	50.8	2,452	44.5	155	2.8	20	.4	86	1.6

*Number of part-time students adjusted downwards by HEW formula based on credit-hours of registered students, preliminary tabulations.

Source: U.S. Department of Health, Education and Welfare, Civil Rights Division.

Table 6-2

Enrollments in the City Colleges of Chicago by Race, October 1968 and 1970, All Students (Including Part-Time) on Each Campus*

City Colleges of Chicago by Campus	Total All Races Number 1968	Total All Races Number 1970	Total All Races Percent 1968	Total All Races Percent 1970	White Number 1968	White Number 1970	White Percent 1968	White Percent 1970	Black Number 1968	Black Number 1970	Black Percent 1968	Black Percent 1970
Amundsen-Mayfair Campus	3,190	3,095	92.5	87.5	2,952	2,683	92.5	86.7	84	154	2.6	5.0
Kennedy-King Campus	4,365	3,442	88.2	65.0	713	182	16.3	5.3	3,592	3,217	82.3	93.5
Loop Campus	6,513	6,869	91.0	82.4	3,275	2,689	50.3	39.1	2,702	3,513	41.5	51.1
Malcolm-X Campus	1,745	3,872	95.4	99.0	312	30	17.9	0.8	1,392	3,810	79.8	98.4
Olive-Harvey Campus	5,368	2,577	86.3	48.1	3,083	788	57.4	30.6	2,102	1,693	39.2	65.7

Southwest Campus	3,193	4,525	70.2	87.7	3,103	4,354	97.2	94.8	35	59	1.1	1.2
Wright Campus	6,146	7,029	79.8	85.7	5,677	6,380	92.4	90.7	178	251	2.9	3.6
All Campuses	30,520	31,409	84.9	80.2	19,115	17,106	62.6	54.5	10,085	12,697	33.0	40.4

City Colleges of Chicago by Campus	Spanish-American				American-Indian				Oriental-American			
	Number		Percent		Number		Percent		Number		Percent	
	1968	1970	1968	1970	1968	1970	1968	1970	1968	1970	1968	1970
Amundsen-Mayfair Campus	79	171	2.5	5.5	17	15	0.5	0.5	58	72	1.8	2.3
Kennedy-King Campus	30	17	0.7	0.5	11	12	0.3	0.3	19	14	0.4	0.4
Loop Campus	376	461	5.8	6.7	19	29	0.3	0.4	141	177	2.2	2.6
Malcolm-X Campus	30	26	1.7	0.7	1	5	0.1	0.1	10	1	0.6	0.0
Olive-Harvey Campus	110	72	2.0	2.7	36	11	0.7	0.4	37	13	0.7	0.4
Southwest Campus	37	74	1.2	1.6	8	9	0.3	0.1	10	29	0.3	0.6
Wright Campus	151	236	2.5	3.4	33	17	0.3	0.2	107	145	1.7	2.1
All Campuses	813	1,057	2.7	3.4	125	98	0.4	0.3	382	451	1.3	1.4

*Actual number of individuals registered on each campus, either as full-time or part-time students, excluding foreign students.

Source: City Colleges of Chicago.

72

Table 6-3

Enrollments in Illinois Institutions of Higher Education by Race and Grade Level, Fall 1970*

All Institutions Public and Private	Total All Races	White		Black		Spanish-American		American-Indian		Oriental-American	
		Number	Percent	Number	Percent	Number	Percent	Number	Percent	Number	Percent
Undergraduate	266,418	238,308	89.4	22,672	8.5	2,095	.8	1,215	.5	2,128	.8
First Year	112,703	97,608	86.6	12,849	11.4	1,114	1.0	379	.3	753	.7
Second Year	68,976	61,757	89.5	5,800	8.4	537	.8	343	.5	539	.8
Third Year	44,756	41,493	92.7	2,307	5.2	245	.5	270	.6	441	1.0
Fourth Year	39,983	37,450	93.7	1,716	4.3	199	.5	223	.6	395	1.0
Nonundergraduate	33,491	30,817	92.0	1,658	5.0	266	.8	62	.2	688	2.1
First Year	16,514	14,877	90.1	1,015	6.1	151	.9	47	.3	424	2.6
Second Year	16,977	15,940	93.9	643	3.8	115	.7	15	.1	264	1.6
All Students	299,909	269,125	89.7	24,330	8.1	2,361	.8	1,277	.4	2,816	.9

*Full-time equivalent basis, preliminary tabulations.

Source: U.S. Department of Health, Education and Welfare, Civil Rights Division.

Table 6-4

Enrollments in Public Community Colleges in the Suburban Ring of Metropolitan Chicago by Race, October 1970.[1]

Public Community Colleges[2]	Total All Races	White		Black		Spanish-American		American-Indian		Oriental-American	
		Number	Percent	Number	Percent	Number	Percent	Number	Percent	Number	Percent
College of Lake County	1,708	1,605	94.0	83	4.9	16	.9	–	–	4	.2
Elgin Community College	1,267	1,229	97.0	21	1.7	12	.9	–	–	5	.4
Joliet Junior College	4,130	3,888	94.1	179	4.3	60	1.5	2	–	1	–
McHenry County College	1,238	1,238	100.0	–	–	–	–	–	–	–	–
Moraine Valley Community College	2,983	2,947	98.8	30	1.0	2	.1	1	–	3	.1
Morton College	1,293	1,288	99.6	–	–	4	.3	–	–	1	.1
Oakton Community College	493	477	96.8	11	2.2	1	.2	2	.4	2	.4
Prairie State College	1,315	1,215	92.4	81	6.2	16	1.2	–	–	3	.2
Thorton Community College	2,129	1,875	88.1	227	10.7	13	.6	9	.4	5	.2
Triton College	3,582	3,073	85.8	476	13.3	33	.9	–	–	–	–
Waubonsee Community College	951	904	95.1	23	2.4	15	1.6	4	.4	5	.5
William Rainey Harper College	3,291	3,262	99.1	7	.2	18	.5	–	–	4	.1
All Colleges	24,380	23,001	94.3	1,138	4.7	190	.8	18	.1	33	.1

[1] Full-time equivalent basis, preliminary tabulations.

[2] Student enrollments in the College of DuPage not available.

Source: U.S. Department of Health, Education and Welfare, Civil Rights Division.

Table 6-5
Enrollments in Chicago State College by Race, Fall 1970*

Grade Level	Total All Races	White Number	White Percent	Black Number	Black Percent	Spanish-American Number	Spanish-American Percent	American-Indian Number	American-Indian Percent	Oriental-American Number	Oriental-American Percent
Undergraduate	3,003	1,204	40.1	1,663	55.4	57	1.9	67	2.2	12	.4
First Year	1,170	340	29.1	787	67.3	25	2.1	14	1.2	4	.3
Second Year	346	169	48.8	164	47.4	4	1.2	9	2.6	—	—
Third Year	936	436	46.6	444	47.4	15	1.6	34	3.6	7	.7
Fourth Year	551	259	47.0	268	48.6	13	2.4	10	1.8	1	.2
All Students	3,003	1,204	40.1	1,663	55.4	57	1.9	67	2.2	12	.4

*Full-time equivalent basis, preliminary tabulations.

Source: U.S. Department of Health, Education and Welfare, Civil Rights Division.

Table 6-6
Enrollments in Northeastern Illinois State College by Race, Fall 1970*

Grade Level	Total All Races	White Number	White Percent	Black Number	Black Percent	Spanish-American Number	Spanish-American Percent	American-Indian Number	American-Indian Percent	Oriental-American Number	Oriental-American Percent
Undergraduate	3,362	2,993	89.0	155	4.6	68	2.0	99	2.9	47	1.4
First Year	1,048	868	82.8	89	8.5	32	3.1	38	3.6	21	2.0
Second Year	774	702	90.7	25	3.2	13	1.7	23	3.0	11	1.4
Third Year	900	821	91.2	24	2.7	15	1.7	29	3.2	11	1.2
Fourth Year	640	602	94.1	17	2.7	8	1.3	9	1.4	4	.6
Nonundergraduate	84	70	83.3	12	14.3	1	1.2	1	1.2	—	—
First Year	84	70	83.3	12	14.3	1	1.2	1	1.2	—	—
All Students	3,446	3,063	88.9	167	4.8	69	2.0	100	2.9	47	1.4

*Full-time equivalent basis, preliminary tabulations.

Source: U.S. Department of Health, Education and Welfare, Civil Rights Division.

teria of selection and performance were also ill-defined. A systematic, objective, statewide or nationwide survey to analyze and compare the success or failure of aspects of these experimental programs is obviously needed. But comparative evaluation may be premature since several of the programs are only two or three years old. Yet, a statewide conference for the purpose, at least, of pooling experiences, tentatively identifying the most effective and economical courses of action, and defining common evaluation criteria in advance would seem propitious.

Apart from special programs for the "disadvantaged," a much larger number of what might be considered "high-risk" students—those with weak academic records or exceedingly low family incomes, including many minority students— are admitted under regular procedures into senior colleges located near impacted poverty areas, as, for example, Southern Illinois University or Chicago State College. At Chicago State, for example, where black enrollments amounted to three-fifths of the total student body, many students were very poor. When comparing the academic records and family incomes of the two hundred or more students enrolled in their experimental "intensive education" program for the "disadvantaged" with those of regular students in the bottom fourth or fifth of the freshman class, they were virtually indistinguishable.

In a real sense, students in the bottom fourth or fifth of the freshman class of most public senior colleges are likely candidates for the extra educational, financial, and counselling supports offered in "special educational opportunity programs" if they are to remain in college and complete their degrees. The high attrition rates in state colleges would suggest this need, and the attrition rates of black students are much higher than those of white students.

Poverty

Despite deficiencies in earlier education and lower than average scores on college entrance examinations, which will be discussed later, many impecunious and many minority students do meet prevailing requirements for college entrance and are highly motivated to attend. The erosion of able students for predominantly financial reasons, however, appears to be enormous.

Recently released statistics from Project Talent, a large-scale, national student survey, revealed that the proportion of even highly qualified students who enter college declines sharply if their parents' incomes are low (Table 6-7). For example, among the most able high school graduates, those ranking in the top fifth of the sample of academic aptitude, only 35% from families in the lowest socio-economic quartile enrolled in college in the first year after graduation and only 50% within five years after graduation. In contrast, among students of com-

Table 6-7
College Entrance[1] by Ability and Socioeconomic Status[2]

Socioeconomic Status Quartile	Number of High School Graduates in Group	Number who Enter College	Talent Loss
Top ability group (100-80%)			
1. High	203,000	192,000 (95%)	11,000 (5%)
2.	153,000	120,000 (79%)	33,000 (21%)
3.	122,000	82,000 (67%)	40,000 (33%)
4. Low	60,000	30,000 (50%)	30,000 (50%)
Totals	538,000	424,000 (79%)	114,000 (21%)
Ability group two (80-60%)			
1. High	130,000	109,000 (84%)	21,000 (16%)
2.	143,000	90,000 (63%)	53,000 (37%)
3.	148,000	78,000 (52%)	70,000 (48%)
4. Low	94,000	34,000 (36%)	60,000 (64%)
Totals	515,000	311,000 (60%)	204,000 (40%)
Total (top 40%)	1,053,000	735,000 (70%)	318,000 (30%)
Ability group three (60-40%)			
1. High	94,000	65,000 (69%)	29,000 (31%)
2.	135,000	63,000 (46%)	72,000 (54%)
3.	159,000	55,000 (34%)	104,000 (66%)
4. Low	148,000	35,000 (24%)	113,000 (76%)
Totals	536,000	218,000 (41%)	318,000 (59%)
Subtotal (1-3 quintiles)	1,600,000	952,000 (60%)	648,000 (40%)

[1] Entrance to college means degree-credit only, within five years of high school graduation.

[2] The probabilities for these tables are derived from unpublished data from "Project Talent," five-year, follow-up survey of the 1960 twelfth and eleventh grade high school students. The 1965-1966 high school graduates in *Digest of Educational Statistics*, 1967, Table 65, were then distributed according to the Project Talent probabilities.

Source: *Toward a Social Report*, U.S. Department of Health, Education and Welfare, Washington, D.C.: 1969.

parable ability from families in the top socioeconomic quartile, 82% enrolled in college within a year after graduation from high school and 95% within five years.[g]

Differences in attendance at graduate and professional schools, five years after high school graduation, are even more marked. Students whose parents are in the top socioeconomic quartile are five times more likely to continue their education beyond the baccalaureate level than those whose parents are in the bottom quartile.[9]

Two conceptions of equality of educational opportunity can be distinguished operationally. First, no student who might wish to attend a postsecondary institution should be denied that opportunity for financial reasons. Second, all students would attend postsecondary institutions in the same proportion as those from upper-income families. The latter definition, in our view, is invalid.

If high school graduates from all socioeconomic levels attended college in the same proportion as those from the top socioeconomic quartile when matched according to tested academic aptitudes, more than half a million additional students would enter college each year. Accordingly, the number entering college would be increased by about one-half in each high school graduating class.

The doubling of college entrance from each high school would, in effect, mean universal higher education, just as we are now beginning to approach universal high school education. Such a goal is not advanced as either attainable or desirable in the next decade. It is questionable whether formal higher education in any of its varied modes is appropriate to the needs and tastes of every youth, including many of the more affluent youths now in college for lack of attractive options. Alternative, rewarding pathways for less scholarly youths are needed, and a number of interesting proposals have been advanced. They include, for example, national or state service corps with built-in education components, cooperative vocational education in a variety of untried forms, or credit-grants for post-high school education, available once to each youth, anytime in his lifetime for any educational purpose, including but not limited to classical forms of higher education.

Kingman Brewster Jr. and Martin Trow have written knowledgeably of the "involuntary student." They suggest that the draft, the social attractions of being exclusively with one's peers in a youth culture, and the necessity to establish credentials for good jobs have made college-going, in effect, compulsory and almost universal at the upper end of the social spectrum. Some of the unrest on campuses may be ascribed to the lack of consonance between the personal values and goals of numerous students and those of scholarly institutions. Accordingly, the disciplinary and institutional problems heretofore found mostly in compulsory lower-school systems have been transferred to college campuses.

[g]According to a Statewide High School Testing Program cited in the Illinois Master Plan (1964), among the upper half of Illinois students, ranked according to tested academic skills, 37% did not go to college; and in Chicago, the proportion was even higher, amounting to 40%.

The first conception of equality of educational opportunity, however, is operationally sound. The choice to pursue advanced education or career training to the full measure of one's capacity clearly should reside with the student himself and without regard to family financial resources. Moreover, the options should be open even in maturity, when, for many individuals, identity and financial problems are often mitigated.

Despite the doubling of college enrollments since 1960, both in Illinois and in the United States as a whole, present facilities are well below latent, undergraduate needs in the near future. Although the aspirations of a growing proportion of low-income students for higher education have been realized, the probability of attending college still remains closely linked with family income (Tables 6-8 and 6-9).

Of the relatively few black students who do manage to go to college, many are plagued by severe financial problems, which partially account for their high attrition rates. Family incomes of college students in the United States, distributed by race are tabulated in Table 6-9. The table reveals that more than half, some 55.5% of black college students in the United States, had family incomes below $6,000, compared with only 14.2% of white students with equally low family incomes. At the upper end of the scale, some 24.7%, or about a quarter of white students came from families with incomes over $15,000, while 5.9% of black students had similarly high family incomes.[h]

Table 6-8
College Attendance of 1966 High School Graduates, by Family Income, February 1967[1]

Family Income	Number of High School Graduates Surveyed	Number Entering College	College Entrance Rates
Under $3,000	268,000	53,000	19.8
$3,000 to $3,999	167,000	54,000	32.3
$4,000 to $5,999	488,000	180,000	36.9
$6,000 to $7,499	367,000	151,000	41.1
$7,500 to $9,999	490,000	250,000	51.0
$10,000 to $14,999	477,000	292,000	61.3
$15,000 and over	160,000	139,000	86.7
Total	2,417,000	1,119,000	46.3

[1] Derived from: "Factors Related to High School Graduation and College Attendance, 1967, "Current Population Reports, Series P-20, No. 185.

Source: *Priorities in Higher Education*, Report of the President's Task Force on Higher Education, U.S. Government Printing Office, Washington, D.C., August, 1970.

[h]The family income of the 37,476 freshmen students in Illinois colleges in 1967 is presented in Table 6-9. While the figures are not strictly comparable, the range of income distribution resembles that of white college students throughout the country shown in Table 6-10. Accordingly, 13.5% of Illinois freshmen came from families with incomes under $6,000 and 23.4% from those with incomes over $15,000.

Table 6-9
Family Income of Freshman Students in Illinois Colleges, 1967

Income	Percent of Total
Less than $4,000	5.4
$4,000-$5,999	8.1
$6,000-$7,999	14.1
$8,000-$9,999	18.6
$10,000-$14,999	29.6
$15,000-$19,999	9.5
$20,000-$24,999	3.8
$25,000-$29,999	1.9
$30,000 or more	3.2
No response	5.8
Total Response	94.2

Source: Illinois Board of Higher Education, *Admission and Retention of Students*, Master Plan: Phase III, Committee B., Springfield: June, 1969.

Table 6-10
Parental Income of United States College Freshmen by Race, 1968

Income	Percent	
	Black	Nonblack
Income less than $4,000	30.7	4.8
$4,000-$5,999	24.8	9.4
6,000- 7,999	17.0	15.4
8,000- 9,999	10.5	16.3
10,000-14,999	10.7	28.2
15,000-19,999	3.4	11.7
20,000-24,999	1.4	5.5
25,000-29,999	0.5	2.7
30,000 or more	0.6	5.0

Source: *Black Students in American Colleges*, American Council on Education, Washington, D.C.: 1969.

Each of the colleges in Illinois, for example, enrolls a significant number of students who require financial assistance if they are to continue their education, but only a few draw appreciable numbers from the lowest socioeconomic stratum. Commuter colleges in populous districts are presumably the most economical mode of higher education, both for the state and for the student, and their expansion was therefore emphasized in state plans, first at lower division levels and subsequently at upper division levels. State scholarships and grants cover tuition costs. Living expenses, books, supplies and other costs must be met through summer or part-time employment, work-study programs, or student loans. In New York State, where living costs are comparable to those in Illinois, it was found that a family income of $9,000 was required in 1967 to meet fully the costs of college attendance at tuition-free institutions.[10]

While the present levels of financial aids in most states may permit working-class students to attend college, they provide insufficient support for qualified and motivated students from truly indigent families. For the latter, their living costs and the earnings that they forego by not working, their "opportunity costs," figure heavily in calculating the real costs that must be borne by them and their families for higher education. The effective cost of attending low tuition or even "free" commuter colleges are much higher than generally estimated if "opportunity costs," living at home, transportation and sundries are included in the balance. This partially accounts for the low college attendance of many talented, impoverished students.[11]

As one ascends the educational ladder, opportunities for commuter students of slender means declines correspondingly in states where the principal public universities are located in rural areas. At the highest graduate and professional levels, one finds, even in Chicago among the several universities serving a region of seven and a half million persons, that high quality, low-cost programs open to qualified commuters are virtually nonexistent in numerous specialized fields, including several intimately related to urban problems. For an adult man or woman who must support a family while studying, the highest reaches of achievement and of the occupational ladder are, in effect, closed off.

Deficient Academic Preparation

Financial problems are only one of several major barriers to higher education for many urban youths. Not only is college more feasible economically for children of upper- and middle-class socioeconomic backgrounds, but they usually receive a better-than-average early education as well. They tend to score better on standard achievement tests and meet academic requirements more easily.

The greatest, single hurdle for the graduates of urban, lower-class high schools is the quality of the education with which they customarily emerge and their shaky mastery of skills and concepts essential to further learning. The failure of many urban schools to reach and teach even their most talented students, much less those of average ability, is a nationwide problem of the highest priority. Part of the problem resides in the school system itself, but its roots are more complex, reaching down into the early family and community setting of educational achievement and development. The community service policies of higher education discussed in later chapters are thus closely linked with those discussed here. cussed here.

Whatever the causes, it is plain that a high proportion of the graduates of urban high schools, segregated by class and race, are foredoomed to academic failure in conventional colleges without considerable special help. Without such help, an open-door admissions policy is little more than a revolving door, leading only to a repetition of earlier frustration and not to higher education.

Because of racial and cultural biases built into standard achievement tests, they do not accurately measure the potential ability of economically deprived, culturally segregated, or rural students. If admission criteria are capricious with regard to predicting the college performance of middle-class students, they are all the more so in the case of students from deficient urban schools. How many students can successfully overcome earlier handicaps remains to be seen, but surely it is prudent social policy to offer all a second chance to learn.

While standard achievement tests may not provide reliable guides to the academic potential of "disadvantaged" students, they nevertheless do reflect better than any other readily available measures the levels in skills acquired in school.[i] They are fairly accurate predictors of scholastic achievement in traditional academic institutions as well. An ability to manipulate verbal and mathematical symbols is essential to the successful pursuit of higher education. Yet, many ambitious and potentially capable students are emerging from high school today with primitive intellectual tools.

To cite an example, test scores of juniors attending high schools in Chicago and their comparative performance, nationally, in reading and arithmetic were released in 1970 by its Board of Education. The average scores attained in each Chicago public high school are presented in Table 2-5, in conjunction with the expressed plans of students after graduation. A marked dysjunction is revealed between the high proportion of students who aspire and plan to go to college and the low proportion of those who are adequately prepared for college, as reflected in the woefully low test scores.

The average junior in comparatively few high schools in Chicago had reading scores anywhere near the national average or above it. The median percentile score for all students tested in Chicago public high schools was 35, well below the 50th percentile which marked the median scores for all students in the nation. The average junior in predominantly black or Spanish-speaking neighborhood high schools was reading at 8th grade level or lower. This means that almost half of his fellow students had not as yet attained even that level of reading facility, although they remained voluntarily in school past the age of compulsory

---

[i]The academic preparation of the students in the City Colleges of Chicago and their scores as measured in the American College Testing Program depart significantly from state and national averages. By way of a rough comparison, the composite score of freshmen at the City Colleges of Chicago was 15 in 1968, which was below average; composite scores in Illinois community colleges of 17.4 are also below the comparable national score of 18. At both Circle Campus of the University of Illinois and Northeastern Illinois State College, the composite scores were 23, which was above the national average of about 20.5 for senior college freshmen. Of the 36,000 students registered at the City Colleges of Chicago in Fall 1969, 20,000 were graduated from the public high schools of Chicago and only 27% had been enrolled in college preparatory curricula.[12]

attendance. What about the skills of the larger number of youths of the same age, in the same neighborhoods, who had already quit high school? About 60% of the young people who enter high schools in Chicago's poverty areas typically leave before graduation, as contrasted with only about 8% in its suburban ring, middle-class high schools.[13] In some schools, median scores were so low as to suggest that functional illiteracy was the norm rather than the exception.

In the light of these findings which are replicated in every major city, the educational responsibilities of the colleges who admit the ill-prepared graduates of urban high school systems are formidable.[j] Even the most gifted and persevering graduates of demonstrated ability, for example, ranking near the top of the class, are likely to encounter academic difficulties on entering senior colleges or universities. If black, the difficulties may be compounded by the cultural shock of being plunged into a middle-class, white environment for the first time. Whereas heretofore, the new college student may have been regarded as distinguished in his home community, viewed as a leader, suddenly, he finds himself an unproven, nonentity in a seemingly hostile, foreign, competitive place. If enrolled in a large, impersonal institution, with complicated administrative procedures and unfamiliar regulations, adjustment will be all the more difficult.

A growing number of the graduates of deficient high schools in urban poverty areas can be expected to enroll in state colleges during the seventies. Good teaching, particularly in the often critical freshman year, is therefore exceedingly important to further progression. And the remediation role assigned to the community colleges is also of increasing significance. It is a pivotal function for many students and one that will grow in scale until urban lower schools are improved.[k]

Attrition

If present trends were to continue, a point would be approached in the next decade when most conventionally qualified minority and indigent students would have ostensible access to one or another institution of higher education.

---

[j]Indeed, the City Colleges of Chicago accept students over 19 years of age without a high school diploma. This is not a universal practice among community colleges even in those states that guarantee college admission to all high school graduates. For example, the recently heralded open-admissions plan of City University of New York assured admission only to all high school graduates.

[k]The magnitude of the future remediation task for Illinois community colleges can only be surmised, but it is clear that a few of the colleges are likely to carry most of the load for the state. In 1969-70, for example, in all public community colleges, a total of 73,000 student-credit-hours were offered in general studies, the euphemism for remedial courses. Almost half of this total, or 32,000 student-credit-hours, were offered in the City Colleges of Chicago. Otherwise, remedial offerings were relatively dispersed, with orders of magnitude ranging from 5,200 hours at Illinois Central in Peoria, downward to 3,000 to 4,000 in Triton, Shawnee, Kaskaskia, Thornton, Danville, with even less at other colleges.

In the light of the current high rates of attrition, perhaps the more fundamental issue for the seventies is whether these students will have access to education itself or only to an educational institution.

The exigencies of rapid expansion have necessarily thrown the spotlight on the barriers to college entrance, while actual educational outcomes have fallen in the shadows. But if the gates to higher education are thrown wide, is it surprising that students with a wide spectrum of ability and personal goals come marching through? What many students find in college is evidently discordant with their goals and needs, judging by the high rates of voluntary exit from open-door state colleges. Barriers to higher education are to be found deeply imbedded in established modes and practices on campus, practices often irrelevant to the learning process itself.

The average rate of attrition or more simply, the percent of students who enter and leave without a degree, from all institutions of higher education is 60%, but variations among different institutions are so great as to render a national average meaningless (Table 6-11). There is obviously, by design, a rather close fit of institution and student in private universities with selective admission policies; about 80-85% of their entering students complete undergraduate degrees in four years, with an additional 10% finishing somewhere else within ten years. The less selective the institution in admissions, however, the higher the rate of attrition and the greater the implied divergence of fit between the education offered and the education pursued by its students. Among students who

Table 6-11
Variation in Graduation Rates According to Selectivity of Institutions

Type of Institution[1]	Percentage of Students Graduating within 4 Years at Initial Institution	Percentage Graduating within 10 Years at Some Institution	1st-time Full-time Enrollments, Fall 1969	Percentage of All 1st-time, Full-time Enrollees
Fifteen most selective private universities	80-85	90-95	20,000	1
Large state universities	35-45	60-70	239,000	15
State colleges	15-25	35-50	322,000	21
Public junior colleges	20-25[2]	15-30[3]	457,000	29

[1] Remaining categories of institutions are: less selective private universities (73,000 first-time enrollees, or 5%); 4-year private colleges (266,000 first-time enrollees, or 17%); 2-year private colleges (55,000 first-time enrollees, or 4%); and small State universities (116,000 enrollees, or 7%), or a total of 1.55 million first-time, full-time enrollees.

[2] Graduation from the 2-year program in a 2-year period.

[3] Graduation with a 4-year degree after transfer.

Source: *Report on Higher Education*, U.S. Department of Health, Education and Welfare, Washington, D.C.: March, 1971.

embark on higher education at community colleges, only 15-30% will continue on to receive a baccalaureate degree somewhere else within ten years. Considering that many community college students would otherwise have been denied any possibility of higher education, the persistence of one in four or five is a genuine accomplishment.

Nevertheless, is it responsible and reasonable social policy to guarantee access to post-high school educational institutions and not simultaneously provide for a plurality of educational options better attuned to the divergent, educational requirements of prospective students?

A comparable question arises within the state colleges that accept many economically, socially, or educationally "disadvantaged" students. More effort has been expended recently in helping new students adjust to college than in exploring the ways that the college itself might adjust to the needs of its varied students. Despite surveys of verbalized, socially acceptable, conventional reasons for withdrawal from college, little is actually known as to the internal trade-offs that might propel a student out, but rates of attrition are much higher among the poor and racial minorities. Although data are fragmentary, it would appear that more than 70% of black freshmen entering four-year colleges do not graduate. Before launching extensive outreach programs, it would seem sensible to investigate why this occurs and what might be done to reduce attrition.[1]

---

[1]In Illinois, Committee B, "On the Admission and Retention of Students," could be reactivated for this purpose and reconstituted to include added representatives of racial minorities.

7 Reducing the Obstacles

If inequalities in access to higher education are to be eradicated, the general lines of action are clear. Some barriers are localized and specific, while others are widespread and involve several kinds of institutions or the system as a whole. Since local priorities and particulars necessarily vary, proposals offered for consideration here are presented in broad outline. Nevertheless, based on direct observation of the effects of current practices, a few strategic lines of action are identified. They largely reflect perceptions of the actual bottlenecks constricting opportunity in Illinois, a state whose public system is already committed to the goal of "extending educational opportunity," the subtitle of its 1966 Master Plan. Proposals of a more comprehensive nature, relating primarily to organizing a systemwide response in metropolitan areas are reserved for the final chapter.

Eliminating Financial Barriers

The most obvious and straightforward way to help qualified students from lower socioeconomic strata attend college is to provide increased financial assistance. All students of demonstrated capacity and need should be assured financial aid to the full extent of their need. The persistence of economic barriers to higher education is unwise, unjust, and short-sighted social policy when balanced against the cumulative social benefits accruing from an educated work force and citizenry. An increase in both the amount and number of scholarships, grants, work-study programs and loans are required just to keep pace with rising tuitions and costs-of-living. If opportunity is to be broadened as well, greatly increased allocations are required to provide for the anticipated future growth in the number of needy and qualified students seeking higher education.

If need is the chief criterion for securing financial aid, a full-scale program of student assistance will be very costly, probably the most costly, single proposal put forward in this study. Federal and state student-aid policies are currently under review in the light of the financial straits of institutions as well as students. Whatever the outcome of these deliberations, it is apparent that over the long pull, a steady annual increase in the overall level of student aids, phased with the anticipated, annual increase in student enrollments is required just to avoid cutbacks. It is estimated that an annual budget increment of 10% is needed by major state universities solely to keep pace with inflation and enrollment growth.[1] Recent tuition increases hit low to middle-income, working-class families hardest and virtually preclude college entrance for students from the lower-income quartile. At major state universities, the median in students' costs, including tuition, fees, room and board, for example, rose by more than 30% between 1966 and 1971. The total pool of financial aids must be increased at a rate more rapid than the anticipated rise in demand by qualified students if opportunity is to be extended beyond its present social boundaries. Otherwise, the competition for limited, available aids will intensify and, as in any zero-sum game, exacerbate urban-rural-suburban, black-white, white-collar, blue-collar tensions.

Besides greatly increasing the aggregate pool of financial aids, the manner in which it is disbursed should be revised so as to promote educational goals for minority students and the poor. In particular, the work in work-study programs can be of a kind that enhances learning and service in poverty areas as well as self-support. In addition, the time-frame in which financial assistance is made available should be far more flexible, enabling students to proceed at their own pace in youth or seek higher education in maturity. Joint work-study scholarships for undergraduates are proposed with supervised precareer training in work places as well as classrooms. Internships and apprenticeships can take many forms, some more appropriate than others to different fields of study, as, for example, concurrent part-time jobs and classes, or sandwich programs with periods of work alternating with periods of study. Paradoxically, only at the graduate level are work and study in special fields typically blended together successfully.

Opportunity Outposts

Decisions about college attendance are usually made at the high school or junior high school level, and good information about career and educational opportunities is often lacking in poverty areas. Nearby colleges and universities have a responsibility (1) to disseminate such information accurately; (2) to reach downward into the schools and assist them in identifying and encouraging promising students; and in some cases, (3) to reach into the community directly so that parents and students may make informed choices and preparations for college.

Rarely are the guidance and counseling services offered at lower-class, urban schools more than perfunctory, and sometimes they are worse, actively misleading and discouraging to insecure, potential college students. When the latter is the case and it is not possible to work effectively through the local school system, alternative channels of information about requirements and financial aids, guidance, counseling, and testing services should be offered directly by the colleges themselves.

Whether they are located on the premises of a community college or university or both, in consortium, supporting a neighborhood outpost will vary according to circumstances, but these kinds of educational services are vitally needed. In densely populated neighborhoods of the inner city, special educational opportunity outposts might be created and widely publicized to make information and services available to the public. Such centers could also serve as a base for related tutorial, after-school recreational, cultural and youth activities, staffed by college students with work-study funds. In sum, colleges and universities should assume responsibility for disseminating information about opportunities and requirements for higher education widely in poverty areas and, when appropriate to the needs of the community, establish opportunity outposts, offering associated educational and youth services, such as testing, counseling and guidance, tutorial, cultural and recreational activities.

Counseling, Advisement, and Service

All successful educational programs for disadvantaged students entail extensive counseling during the first year or two of college, both with regard to personal or family problems and academic or administrative requirements. Many more students have need of such services than presently receive them, including a large sector of the bottom quartile, economically and academically, of the freshman class. Black students coming from segregated high schools, in particular, need good counseling and guidance services on entering large senior institutions. The high cost and shortages of trained counselors, especially black advisors, have been successfully met at City University in New York by employing and training junior faculty and graduate students to perform some of these functions. A modification of this approach to suit other situations suggests itself, through creating an alternative to teaching assistantships to support graduate studies.

Special funds should be allocated to universities to support minority students in graduate and professional schools, and should be offered in the form of counseling assistantships or community project assistantships. The recipients of the assistantships would be expected to offer either (1) part-time, counseling and tutorial services to lower division minority students; or (2) to work with undergraduates, senior faculty, and local neighborhood groups in staffing collaborative community projects, as, for example, the opportunity outposts or others suggested in later chapters.

The assistantships would serve several purposes concurrently. First, the ranks of black students and those of other minority groups noticeably thin out in the upper reaches of the university, and there is an acute nationwide shortage of well-trained, black faculty members and professionals in almost every field. By offering more liberal financial support to minority graduate students in their early years of study, it can be expected that the shortage will be reduced in the future.

Secondly, the paucity of black and minority faculty means that younger students find few successful role models on campus with whom to identify and consult. In universities located in semirural settings especially, the prevailing white, middle-class ambience of the campus and countryside is untempered and uncomfortable for youths who have grown up in a socially heterogeneous, urban atmosphere. Counseling assistantships would be emphasized in semirural universities, and the recruitment of both undergraduates and graduate students from underrepresented minority groups would be undertaken, in tandem, for the purpose of desegregating the campus.

Third, for urban universities, the firsthand knowledge of both graduate and undergraduate students from poverty areas is an invaluable asset in community projects, which can be turned to simultaneous advantage for the university, the student, and the community area. Conceivably, scholarships for supervised work in specified fields could also be offered to undergraduates in the form of traineeships. It is often found that educationally disadvantaged students may need more time than four years to mature intellectually. Scholarships combining purposeful, socially useful work with reduced course loads could greatly increase the probability of their completing their degrees, even if it might take five to seven years.

Fostering Innovations in Teaching and Learning

Good teaching during the first year of college is important for all students, but for the graduates of urban lower-class, segregated high schools, it is often crucial to future progression. For the latter, varied teaching styles to conform to diverse learning styles are needed in the beginning until students have learned how to teach themselves independently. The small classes and revised course materials offered in some of the "special educational opportunity programs" might be made available as options for a limited period to otherwise qualified students. During this time of fiscal retrenchment when extensive outreach and recruitment programs are precluded, for the short run, efforts to identify and eliminate the causes of the high attrition rates among students already admitted from urban poverty areas are to be emphasized.

Large universities and colleges are moving away from mass courses and standardized curricula toward creating smaller, discrete, collegiate subunits to provide diversified educational options, teaching styles, and, flexibility for individual students. Opportunities for off-campus study are increasing, with many more formal courses focused sharply on the problems of the contemporary world. The service projects discussed in later chapters feed into these kinds of educational adaptations.

There is no substitute, however, for superior teaching, and it is an essential ingredient to the intellectual flowering of students from deficient high schools.

Yet, introductory courses are often relegated to the low man on the totem pole. Good teaching, apparently, like virtue, must be its own reward, since few others have been forthcoming in academia. Academic rank and salaries traditionally bear little relation to faculty teaching strengths, which are unevenly distributed. Each college should explore ways of systematically evaluating undergraduate teaching and provide alternative, additional channels to reward and stimulate outstanding teaching. Since revision and updating of course curricula and pedagogical methods take time, special grants or released time for faculty and faculty workshops, including doctoral candidates expecting to teach, might be made available for this purpose.

Faculty and students with a zest for new undertakings can be directly encouraged to grapple with practical problems in poverty areas by the chief administrators of an institution. The climate for innovation and its support is created in a variety of ways, depending on the size, mission and internal structure of an institution. Leadership, with supplementary channels and funds, must often be provided by the administration itself to give a hearing to, incubate and test new educational programs, at least long enough to discern their probable viability. Otherwise, many new ideas are unlikely to survive the hard labor of passing through innumerable, established faculty committees. Innovation need not be the sole, dominant mode of an institution. As suggested by one college president, "All too often the grand-scale experiment leads to rapid institutionalization of a few new ideas which become old very fast."[a]

Whatever the ways—and money, time and prestige are most effective—faculty and students who lend their efforts to new ventures should not have to bear the costs personally, as they often do. Alternatives to the established reward systems in universities need to be developed expressly to foster and recognize such contributions. For example, while academic rank might be determined according to traditional criteria and procedures, salary increments within rank might take account of extraordinary contributions.

The professional advancement of faculty members is determined largely by peers in their profession or discipline. Apart from personal satisfactions, which may be great, participation in new educational or problem-solving endeavors may or may not enhance professional standing. Depending on the project, it may lend new perspectives to research, leading to new insights and publications, but perhaps not. Surely, at the least, they should not be penalized for participation in innovative and therefore risky educational or community projects. As Florence Nightingale remarked long ago, "Whatever else hospitals do, they should not spread infection." And whatever else higher education does, it should not inhibit innovations or endeavors conducive to new knowledge or practice.

[a]At Northeastern Illinois State College, for example, the Office of Program Development was established as a vehicle for promoting experimentation. According to its president, Dr. Jerome M. Sachs, "A director and advisory committee pass on proposals and give time limits and evaluation standards. An unusual program does not need to go through the complete routine of curriculum council approval until there is sufficient expertise to be able to substantiate the promise of success." The quote in the text is also his.

A Second Chance to Learn in
Community Colleges

The community college is a frontier of higher education, one that holds great promise for interrupting intergenerational poverty. Largely by default, the urban colleges located near poverty areas have had vital new social functions thrust upon them. The community college should not be the sole vehicle of higher education for a black student or an impecunious student, but it has rapidly become the dominant one.

Apart from remedial course work per se, extra counseling and guidance, skill centers to permit individual progression, testing, health and other allied educational services are generally needed. But above all, a pragmatic stance toward teaching and neighborhood problems is essential, geared expressly to students in poverty areas who have been unresponsive to conventional education. Some community colleges, all-black or all-chicano, have made an educational virtue of the necessity imposed by de facto segregation and emphasize race consciousness as the key to motivation and learning. Others, with the conviction that the separation of liberal from practical education is artificial for their students, have developed programs in which vocational education is not regarded as a stepchild but rather a stepping stone to conceptualization and intellectual insights, hiring adjunct faculty with practical skills as needed. Whatever the particular mode, the essential ingredient is superior, responsive teaching and a comprehensive, fresh approach to the development of the student.

Devising innovative pedagogical methods, including unexplored forms of apprenticeship and cooperative education in technical and human service fields, entails extensive experimentation. Faculty workshops and in-service training, new curricula designs and approaches are time-consuming, requiring an infusion of creative talent and money.

Because of the geographic concentration of racial minorities and of poverty, responsibilities are unevenly distributed among the community colleges in any state, the highest costs generally falling upon those districts with the heaviest demands on tax dollars for public services. Extra resources are needed in those community colleges which are, in essence, pioneering on the edges of pedagogical knowledge and social change. Additional state funds, beyond those allocated under standard formulas that match local with state contributions, should be provided to the community colleges drawing students from the lowest socioeconomic levels.[b]

Since the community college is the frequent point of entry into higher education for the poor, a second set of problems emerges relating to the articulation

---

[b]In Illinois, the City Colleges of Chicago, East St. Louis, Illinois State, Shawnee and several others have borne the major responsibility in the state for offering opportunity to the educationally indigent. Further proposals relating to statewide coordination and funding of programs for the poor in community colleges are presented in the final chapter.

of its programs with senior colleges and universities. Even with new modes of teaching and learning, common standards of achievement must prevail to facilitate upward mobility and transfers from junior to senior institutions.

If the open-door community college is to fulfill its strategic educational role in the system, opportunities for lateral and upward movement by able students should be relatively unimpeded. Yet students who attend community colleges and successfully complete course work which presumably parallels the freshman and sophomore years in senior colleges, often encounter unexpected obstacles in the new college. The extent to which their course work in community colleges will be accredited is often unknown in advance of enrollment. On the average, students are likely to lose about a half a year of credit in transition because they discover too late that "general education" courses and introductory courses in specialized fields are evidently not of the same scope or rigor as those offered in senior colleges and, therefore, not acceptable to the new institution.

Senior institutions should take the initiative to work closely with community colleges to eliminate as far as possible such needless dysjunctions which, in fact, victimize the unknowing student. In addition, the rites of passage for transfer students should be eased in every possible way. Freshman orientation programs are offered in every senior college, but there are none of any consequence for transfer students in the junior year. The faculties of universities which have special strengths in particular departments should consult with neighboring community college faculties to jointly develop acceptable curricula and staff in-service workshops. Joint registration by community college students for specialized course offerings in nearby senior institutions should also be facilitated.

Many examples of cooperative endeavors between senior and junior institutions can be found; but the network of community colleges has expanded so rapidly that serious articulation and communication problems remain unresolved. Public senior institutions should be formally charged with the responsibility to consult with community colleges to eliminate needless obstacles for transfer students and to develop curricula of a quality and scope acceptable to both. Statewide guidelines for this effort should be formulated; special state funds should be made available; and faculty designated in each major division should be given the responsibility for liaison.

Continuing Adult Education

For employed youths and adults or housewives, part-time study may be the only feasible way to continue their education. Opportunities for many kinds of study tend to evaporate as the years pass. Mature women seeking reentry into the labor market after raising a family and adult working men seeking a change of occupation, both encounter similar institutionalized rigidities and arbitrary restrictions, making a mockery of the vision of a mobile learning society. The number of mature men and women seeking higher education will undoubtedly increase during the coming decade for the many reasons indicated earlier. Colleges and universities should be geared to meet these demands with a broader range of curriculum offerings than in the past and with much more flexibility in admissions and in scheduling courses at times, ways, and places appropriate to adults. If the tuitions charged are expected to cover the cost of the course work, financial aids on the basis of demonstrated need should be available to part-time, matriculated, mature students as well as to youthful day students.

The community colleges are well-suited to respond to local civic needs, cultural and recreational tastes, and broad educational interests, with part-time, low-cost, round-the-clock, round-the-calendar, credit and noncredit courses. The lectures, seminars, conferences, cultural, recreational and leadership training courses offered can contribute much to community life. Usually, community colleges are also conveniently located and reasonably well-equipped to meet most of the demands for lower division, credit courses and career programs. By the end of the decade, it is probable that the latter sorts of courses will be available to adults in every corner of those states aggressively building up community college networks.

Opportunities for advanced or specialized study on a part-time basis, however, are much more limited everywhere, as is the need. However, a growing demand from employed adult men and women for upper-division, graduate and professional studies can be anticipated. The very success of the community colleges in meeting local, educational needs will, in itself, breed a cadre of new candidates for advanced higher education in specialized fields.

Despite the wide range of extension courses and services presently offered by state colleges and universities, gaps can be discerned, even in major metropolitan areas large enough to permit a comprehensive array of studies.[2] This is less the case in coastal cities than in middle-American cities such as Chicago, where state universities have evolved from land-grant colleges in locations unrelated to population centers. Studies in all professional, technical, liberal arts, and career fields should be possible for adults in major cities as well as for the recent high school graduates towards whom they have been primarily oriented.

The needed expansion of opportunities for low-cost graduate and professional education in nonresidential, urban universities runs counter to current projections of future excess capacity in several graduate fields. A maldistribution of resources is at the bottom of the problem. Consequently, the process of expansion must be highly selective, with relocation of facilities to urban institutions appropriate in some cases and cutbacks in others. A consortium of public senior institutions in major metropolitan areas should be created for the purpose of building a comprehensive network of low-cost, part-time adult education credit courses at upper division and graduate levels.[c] To avoid duplication and future

[c]In Chicago, the Circle Campus of the University of Illinois is ideally situated to take responsibility for identifying and filling out notable gaps in opportunities for advanced studies. The university presently has no formal night school or extension program on any scale, and its centrally located, excellent campus is underutilized in the evenings.

excess capacity, priorities of need will have to be determined in consultation with private universities offering evening degree programs. The responsibility for initiating courses in new fields can be divided among the institutions in accordance with their particular missions, faculty strengths, and interests. Similar consortia including private as well as public colleges are feasible in less populous regions.

The university without walls is another way to promote lifelong access to higher education in both rural and urban settings and to introduce far greater individual flexibility. Several promising new varients of off-campus studies and external degree programs have recently been developed. There is nothing particularly new about the idea of accredited, self-directed studies, only the contemporary comprehensive forms in which it might be packaged and, hopefully, the quality and scope.

Similar in conception to the newly founded open university in Great Britain, recent proposals generally incorporate technological innovations, such as cable TV and electronic cassettes, and involve adjunct faculty drawn from the ranks of practitioners as well as from the highest echelons of academia. Self-directed studies are usually combined with short periods of on-campus counseling, tutorials, and examinations. Although the establishment of a regional examining university would provide an additional way for students to receive formal accreditation for knowledge and skills, however acquired over the course of their lives, the limitations inherent in a system that might necessarily emphasize testable knowledge are evident (particularly if the examining university were the only vehicle for continuing education).

Proposals for regional examining universities or regional TV universities have been embraced with great enthusiasm in many quarters. Several states, including Massachusetts and New York, have already launched statewide experiments in external degree granting universities. For specific details, the reader is referred to the burgeoning discussion on the subject.[3]

Toward Diversity, Integrity and Integration

Students and the general public often ascribe differences in status and quality to the education offered in community colleges, senior colleges, and universities when, in fact, such views may be unwarranted in the light of the students' goals. Higher status is sometimes even accorded to fields of study within institutions. For example, office and business fields are commonly endowed with more prestige than technical and manipulative fields, when actually, at entry levels into the occupational hierarchy, the latter may be more demanding and offer swifter access to good jobs. The prestige accorded a college appears largely to reflect the degree of selectiveness in its admission policies, which does not necessarily mirror what transpires educationally on its campus or its suitability to the personal objectives of a particular student. In the coming decade, the community college can make a unique, unprecedented and vital social contribution if it resists the temptation to become a faithful image of the traditional liberal arts college.

In extending educational opportunity to a wider spectrum of urban society, the invidious and often invalid comparisons among colleges will disappear only if, in reality, each institution is truly excellent in distinctive ways. The aim is a plural system of autonomous colleges and universities, each superior in different areas and with defined characteristics, able to attract students and faculty of similar intellectual and professional concerns. Students, aware of specialized strengths, would then deliberately seek out the colleges that conforms to their own goals and values.

In great cities with several institutions of higher learning, in particular, it is neither sensible nor possible for all public colleges to offer programs in every field. Nor would it be desirable in terms of the indirect secondary social effects that would result from a homogenized educational system. The geography of segregation by class and race in the residential neighborhoods of the region has made integration in the common schools extremely difficult. The educational problems and socioeconomic pattern of enrollment in secondary schools are gradually being transferred upward into the community and senior colleges in metropolitan areas. It may be possible to intervene and actively resist the trend toward stratification and segregation in higher education and the drift toward superior and inferior colleges. Excellence through specialization is one of the ways. If, for example, courses of study in criminal justice or urban planning are offered only in a limited number of places, students of different backgrounds and race will seek them out, and a more varied, social mix will result.

The educational role of each college and university in a state system should be clearly defined; differentiated in terms of particular faculty, departmental, and curriculum strengths; and autonomous in order to pursue its distinctive purpose with individuality and integrity. Standards of educational achievement and excellence should be uniform so that students can transfer laterally and upwards with ease. The scale and complexity of public systems, however, permit a variety of ways, within and among institutions, to attain excellence in teaching and learning. This is an invaluable asset in finding new solutions to all problems.

Part Three:

8 Extending Services to the Urban Poor

Colleges and universities engage in a great many public service activities and relatively few benefit the urban poor. In reaching out to the communities of the poor, what sorts of endeavors should be emphasized and how should they be organized? If the objective is to assure that a child born into poverty need not remain poor, many points of entry into the cycle of poverty, other than higher education itself, are appropriate to centers of higher learning. Not only are prospects for higher education remote, but many of the children of the poor face a lifetime with dim prospects even for steady employment. In this and the next two chapters, the direct relationships of communities of scholars and educators and communities of the poor are explored: (1) as potential purveyors of valuable professional services; and (2) as large institutions with campuses and corporation functions.

Policy Guidelines

In considering community service in the urban slum, a simplistic approach would be attractive, but unfortunately, the experience of the last decade with countless unproductive urban and poverty programs argues otherwise. A growing body of experience is available, however. More has been learned about what not to do than what to do; yet, there is near consensus about some of the lessons of the recent past. To bring about significant improvements in the living conditions of the urban poor, several key elements have emerged which provide guidelines to future service programs in the inner city.

First, any approach to community development must be many-sided. An obvious dictum, it is one more honored in the breach than in the observance. An inadequate income flow and unemployment are at the center of a constellation of other self-reinforcing problems, which include illiteracy and low educational achievement, poor nutrition, slum housing, ill health, delinquency, broken families and anomie. The effectiveness of any single target program tends to be submerged in a tide of concurrent problems, so that whatever the focus of a particular project, other supportive services will be required. In short, if social problems are interrelated, policy responses should be coordinated.

Second, poverty is not, in essence, a neighborhood problem even though its manifestations are localized. Nor can it be addressed effectively by relying exclusively on community, neighborhood, family, or individually focused programs. The chief resources and responsibility for reducing poverty and resolving problems concentrated in the slum are to be found at metropolitan, state and federal levels. By implication, efforts to resolve problems should be directed to their source as well as their symptoms, and the sources of many problems of the poor are rooted in prevailing institutionalized behavior. The quantity and quality of neighborhood services offered the poor are nevertheless exceedingly important to life in the inner city since personal, family and community resources are so limited. Colleges and universities are a potential link between the problems of the neighborhood and the resources and institutions of the greater society.

Third, although vehicles of participation will vary, the inhabitants of poverty areas must be actively involved in planning for community improvement. The motive force for significant social change comes from enlisting the target population in programs of self-help and community development. When this has not transpired, well-intentioned public programs such as housing rehabilitation or compensatory educational projects have produced only surface changes or even backfired. In contrast, pervasive changes in attitudes and living conditions have been brought about when community groups were committed to support of the same programs. For black and Spanish-speaking minorities especially, self-determination and community identity are a crucial component of healthy development and a positive defense against the humiliations of discrimination.

Alternative Approaches

With these perspectives, what sort of service programs should be undertaken by colleges and universities in poverty areas? Three possible general approaches can be discerned.

First, higher education could simply increase the level and redirect the focus of its present public service and extension programs. For example, more Afro-American cultural events might be scheduled. The expansion of nutritional and youth programs into the urban slum under cooperative agricultural extension might be accelerated. The fees for noncredit extension courses in poverty areas might be eliminated, and the subjects offered might better reflect the concerns of the community, as for example, consumer education, property maintenance, black history, parliamentary procedures, or leadership training. Rehabilitation services, legal aid, and hospital outpatient clinics might be enlarged in poverty areas. Surely, the urban slum is lacking the gamut of services and has limitless capacities to absorb whatever is offered. Surely, these are established and excellent services which can and must be adapted to contemporary needs. Many public and private agencies are doing just this, and higher education could run with the pack, leaving the matter at that.

Conventional approaches to community development by other public and private agencies through extending services, however, thus far have had little impact in the inner city. A host of agency programs recently aimed at the slum have brought few observable improvements in living conditions. To the contrary, they frequently tend to reinforce structured dependency.

The reasons advanced for these failures are many. Obviously, the magnitude of existing programs is miniscule and out of scale with the huge pool of human needs. In addition, particular programs may have been badly administered or staffed by inefficient people insensitive to the requirement of clients whose class and cultural style differed from their own. Well-trained personnel are scarce in several professional fields and in local government. "It is axiomatic that services for poor people are most often poor services—poorly run, poorly regarded, and thus poorly used."[1] While these factors do prevail and do affect the outcome of programs, they are not universal, nor can they completely account for the low proportion of successful programs. Indeed, human and public-service occupations tend to attract people with deep-seated, social concerns and sensibilities. And the level of public expenditures in health, welfare, and education has risen significantly in many cities and states.

The question therefore arises as to what extent poverty would be reduced if programs offering services to the poor were separated from income-maintenance disbursements and were adequately funded and excellently administered? Although no a priori answer is possible, the likelihood of making significant inroads on poverty with service programs as presently designed is problematic. The prospects are dubious in our judgment because of deficiencies inherent in the present system which disregards the consumer.

What is nearly universal and characteristic of institutional services is the fragmented, inconvenient and unresponsive manner in which they are dispensed to the poor. The channels through which agencies make their services available to people, such as health care, legal aid, family counselling, housing or employment services, are commonly called delivery systems. These rigid, outmoded delivery systems, or more accurately, when referring to the collection of separate, categorical, functional programs that are extant, the nonsystem, are one of the major bottlenecks in effective service programs.

Service functions in fields such as health, education, law, and social services are now organized "vertically" along professional hierarchies. Official agencies in these fields have high orders of independence, frequently beyond central executive control; they are generally distinguished by elaborate decentralized devices or jurisdictions which nevertheless are limited by the traditional boundaries of the professional activity; and they are universally characterized by requiring the beneficiaries of their services to make whatever accommodations are dictated by the customs of the respective professions or agencies. The pernicious consequences of this situation on the availability of services are far-reaching.

Take, for example, the case of a youngster who does badly in school and is at the point of dropping out. There should be some simple way for his difficulty to be understood, and for something to be done about it, but there isn't. His problem might be an educational one, but there is very little that his teacher will be able to do for him, and seldom any special assistance or tutoring available. His problem may be an emotional one, but psychiatric help is rare, and referral to a clinic from the schools is even more so. His problem may be medical, but to receive help he or his parents would have to recognize the nature of the problem, and seek out a clinic or doctor, a harder task in some communities than in others. His problem may be environmental, that he has no place at home to work since his whole family lives in two rooms, but it is extremely unlikely that better living quarters can be had. Or, more usually, his problem will be a combination of several of these factors, and treatment of any one of the problematic elements will not be enough to break the cycle. Professions which confront this sort of problem with carefully defined areas of operation, intricate bureaucratic paths which must be followed, and poor communication among the agency hierarchies, provide little hope that such problems can be met.[2]

In the light of the acknowledged ineffectiveness, rigidities and petty jurisdictional tyrannies in many health, educational and human service programs, it would seem imprudent to pour resources into conventional channels without re-examining them.

Conceivably higher education could do better, and a second approach to community service, one that flows logically from failures of the first, suggests itself. Colleges and universities might open up their own comprehensive network of coordinated service outposts, paralleling existing service agencies.

Apart from the expense of such outposts, a serious consideration at this juncture, there is no evidence to suggest that the faculties and administrators of colleges would be better managers of comprehensive programs, nor are they necessarily more humane, wise, flexible, efficient or tough-minded than others. Nor is there any convincing evidence that they might succeed where others have failed, in overcoming their own deeply entrenched guild patterns merely by plighting common cause to the needs of the inner city.

Faculty may have considerable technical knowledge, judgment and creative vision in some fields and best of all, a core of enthusiastic youths to enlist voluntarily in service programs. But so long as the policies, style and staffing of projects are determined exclusively by college faculty, there is a strong probability that new service projects would be no less rigid and circumscribed in interest or mission than existing ones. Furthermore, from the standpoint of the poor, the experts from academia would merely be substituting their own tyrannies and perspectives for those of the public bureaucracies and professions.

Granted that human services are rendered in a bewildering variety of ways that in no way correspond to the needs of their beneficiaries, and granted that the fundamental flaw in conventional ways of dispensing services is in the delivery system itself, (or more precisely, the array of separate functional subsystems operating in the urban slum), is the issue simply one of coordination, difficult as that may be? Is it largely a question of bringing together all agency services under a single roof? Coordination, of course, is one of the basic aims of Model Cities and of the "services supermarket" recently proposed by Secretary of Health, Education and Welfare, Eliot H. Richardson.[a]

The nub of the problem, in our view, going beyond coordination, is that crucial policy decisions are made exclusively by the service agencies themselves and that they are made outside the target areas. Enlarging the scale of services, therefore, tends mostly to perpetuate professional power and to reinforce prevailing practices and judgements. Yet, it is precisely the latter that most need overhauling, specifically the health system, the school system, the welfare system, criminal justice, and many other public and human services. They have almost ceased to function in the inner city in terms of achieving presumed aims, such as teaching children to read or lowering mortality or morbidity rates or reducing dependency. Consequently, even if funds were available, it would seem ill-advised for universities or colleges to set up their own service outputs, however comprehensive or excellently administered, if they were to embody the same essential features as existing ones.

In the poverty areas of the inner city, the imperfections in public and human service systems are most exposed, but their performance is less than satisfactory for society as a whole. The glaring deficiencies in black communities, coupled with the current thrust towards self-determination and community development, suggest that inner-city ghettoes are the ideal setting in which to experiment with new kinds of consumer-oriented models for rationalizing the delivery of human services.

A third approach to community service, the one that is advocated here, is for centers of higher learning to concentrate their limited resources for service programs on exploring new ways of promoting community development in poverty areas. By concentration on the design, development and implementation of new models for delivering services, higher education could simultaneously be probing new ways of improving professional practice, knowledge and education. The very activities that higher education is presumably best equipped to perform are those most needed in urban community service programs. Since prevailing professional models in teaching, medicine, social work, urban planning and other

---

[a]Coordination is also a prime objective of two new, state-sponsored projects conducted under the auspices of the recently established Illinois Institute for Social Policy. The State of Illinois established this new Institute in 1970 for the purposes of carrying out research and demonstration projects, focusing on public welfare programs and related areas, such as manpower and health services. The General Assembly appropriated $3,300,000 of research funds within the budget of the Illinois Department of Public Aid for the annual operation of the Institute. Two centers, one in the Woodlawn community area of Chicago and another in Peoria, have been created to house under common roof and aegis the numerous heretofore scattered agencies serving local residents, those providing, for example, health care, welfare payments, manpower training or employment services. Another promising innovation in the design of these projects is the separation of the income-maintenance and payment disbursement aspects of public aid from the social service, family service, and counseling functions. The basic purpose of these experimental centers is to find ways to reduce welfare rolls and dependency.

fields are unsatisfactory in poverty areas, new service and developmental models must be devised and tested.

The central focus of community ventures should be the consumer, the ultimate beneficiary of public and private services, whether an individual, family or community group, according to circumstance. If objectives and results are to be evaluated in terms of the consumer, a frame of reference is provided for reviewing and revising traditional, professional practices and related training programs.

Colleges and universities are uniquely suited to do this for two reasons. First, the fact that they are not operating agencies charged with heavy, day-to-day responsibility for delivering services in gross quantities means that they can pick strategic points of entry into the community. Second, in every field significant to human and community development, one or another institution has special faculty strengths, scholarly interests, and often responsibility for professional education or the training of auxiliary personnel. No single institution embraces all of the component elements needed for a systematic approach to the developmental problems of the slum. But considered together as a system of higher education, a comprehensive array is achieved.[b]

The comprehensiveness of the system as a whole in many states coupled with the lack of comprehensiveness in individual institutions, has several implications. It highlights the need for extensive, interinstitutional cooperation if new and more effective service models, geared to resolving a wide range of interlocking problems, are to be developed. Thus, for example, professional schools with high competency and faculty-student interest in a single field, let us say criminal justice at a law school, could lend assistance to a narrowly focused project. It could be expected that once a program was underway, correlated programs would be grafted on, involving other professions or institutions such as a school of social work or a community college for vocational education.

As suggested earlier, the central organizing principle of community service endeavors should be the needs of a community group as perceived by them. The direction of flow in decision-making and accountability would thus be reversed, so that the target group (rather than the college) becomes the chief point of reference. The responsibility for managing service projects also should reside in the community group to ensure its autonomy and that of the college or university.

The skills and resources to be found in a college or university would be called into play in many and hopefully, new ways if a close working relationship can be achieved. Faculty and students can serve in a variety of roles as consultants,

[b]In the Chicago area, for example, Northeastern Illinois State College and Chicago State College have special competencies in education, the University of Illinois Medical School in health fields, and its Circle Campus in a range of disciplines and professional fields, including urban planning, engineering, business administration and social work. The community colleges in the city and suburbs provide training in numerous, semiprofessional and technical fields. In other, less populous parts of Illinois and in other regions, the configurations of institutional and faculty strengths are, of course, different.

teachers and part-time staff. They might be drawn into the process of community development at every stage, in helping the client define objectives, in identifying likely sources of financial support, in training personnel, in devising new techniques or adaptations, and in developing evaluation criteria. From the standpoint of a community area, service to the target group would be rendered in a more effective and dignified manner. From the standpoint of a particular college, professional school, or department, teaching and research would be infused with new vigor. Research projects could be more finely attuned to phenomena and problems actually encountered. The combination of theory in classroom or library and practice in the field can make teaching and learning a lively process of discovery for all participants.

The educational implications of shifting the seat of responsibility and accountability in community projects from the producers to the consumers of services are extensive. If professional practices and education are to be judged in terms of their impact and outcomes, many necessarily will be called into question as ineffective, inefficient, anachronistic, and even counterproductive. The challenge of promoting development in the urban slum is thus seen as the take-off point for reexamining the very structure of the professions and of professional education. Institutions of higher education, forming the bridge between community groups and the professions, can be catalysts to deep-seated, long-overdue systemic changes.

In this spirit, the current practice which demands that beneficiaries of services adjust their behavior to the dictates of the professions, is replaced . . . by the requirement that the professions and agencies adapt their behavior to the needs of the community . . . each profession (must) reexamine its own professional content and activity to separate those functions which constitute its special skills from those functions which are merely the result of historical accumulation and administrative inertia. In addition, each profession will find new horizons for commitment to functions which are not exclusively oriented toward service, but are rather directed toward training and changing institutional practice.[3]

In short, community service for the urban poor becomes much less a question of dispensing specific services than of generating a process of institutional change. New forms of communication, representation and public accountability are involved. A variety of alternative models for effectively delivering services (both within and across professional fields) must be tested. The process entails exploring new professional roles and career ladders for residents of urban poverty areas. It means mounting new kinds of research and demonstration projects, both interdisciplinary and within specific fields, with teaching and service elements. Lastly, improved techniques of policy analysis are called for, with predetermined evaluation criteria built into each community project.

The proposed approach to community service is neither as abstract nor grandiose as its preliminary exposition might suggest. In actuality, it represents a synthesis of a great many ongoing, disparate trends already emergent in contemporary higher education. They need only to be systematically organized, enlarged, and funded for a comprehensive attack on the problems of the poor. To illustrate more concretely what might be involved programmatically, an example is given in Appendix C, describing the evolution of a typical, small-scale project, a child-care center.

9 The Professions and Systemic Reform

A prime mission of centers of higher learning is the education of professional manpower across the spectrum of employment. An orientation toward practice, toward learning for the sake of doing, and toward the social applications of knowledge has long characterized education in the established professions. Consequently, the role of the professional schools and of the colleges in preprofessional education assumes special significance in the context of service and community projects. In this chapter, these roles are addressed from a variety of standpoints, first from that of the poor and next from that of the colleges.

In particular, two themes running throughout this study converge on the question of training professional personnel to work and render services effectively to the urban poor. The first relates to the malfunctioning (and virtual breakdown) of the health care, human services, and educational systems as they are presently constituted in the urban slum. The second theme relates to the issue of extending educational and employment opportunities to those shut out of our economic system. Both issues are intertwined in a circular relationship. Employment and educational prospects for many of the urban poor, particularly for able-bodied, unemployed youths, underemployed minorities, and female heads of families are tied to the quality of public services made available in poverty areas. Both their immediate prospects, in a remedial sense, and their intergenerational chances for mobility, in a preventative sense, are closely linked with the quality of professional services offered in schools, health centers, correctional institutions, employment agencies, welfare agencies and the like.

Public programs for the unemployed and underemployed usually reflect the interrelationship. Manpower training programs aimed at upgrading skills to fill existing jobs, either in private industry or public agencies, generally entail supportive, auxiliary services. Other poverty programs, however, have addressed both issues simultaneously and both sides of the labor market, creating jobs as well as training people to fill them. Several have incorporated the concept of creating jobs in the public sector to employ the poor directly, most often, in delivering services in their own community.

The first of such programs was launched in the mid-sixties under the auspices of the Office of Economic Opportunity (OEO), but the approach was subsequently reaffirmed in the Public Service Careers Program (PSC). The rise in unemployment in 1970 elicited new federal and state programs with similar features for public service employment. "Hire now, train later" was a central concept in the early OEO programs, the PSC, and the most recent state and federal programs.

105

What is significant to education institutions, of course, is the train later aspect of these programs, and urban community colleges have been developing appropriate educational sequences in collaboration with public agencies. Of foremost significance, however, are the indirect effects flowing from the infusion of new kinds of manpower into the human service professions. Challenging and unresolved issues about the structure of the professions and of professional education have risen to the surface.

Paraprofessionals, Entry and Mobility

A large corps of indigenous community workers, or self-styled "new careerists," has already been created under the auspices of various poverty programs. Several hundred thousand community workers are now employed in the lower echelons of the professions, working as teacher aides, police aides, legal assistants, mental health associates, social work technicians, urban planning technicians, building inspector aides, library aides, recreation assistants, and child-care assistants, to name but a few. The New York City public schools, to cite an example, employed 14,070 community residents in 1971, mostly women and 55% of them black, as teacher, school, and community aides. Begun in fall 1967, the program cost $60 million annually and has been financed largely with federal funds.[1]

The ranks of paraprofessionals in the human services have swelled rapidly in less than five years with good reason. Not only were new employment opportunities offered to the poor, not only were hard-pressed professionals relieved of many routine tasks, but above all, it was found that neighborhood people frequently communicated better with neighborhood clients. They provided a heretofore missing and vital link between the middle-class professional worker and the poor. More than a link, the community worker often assumed the role of a route man, directing traffic into appropriate professional channels, each specialized, unfamiliar or confusing to the client who had a problem. Consider for example, a truant who remains at home, not because of school problems, but because her mother is sick or alcoholic and needs help with the younger children. The immediate problem should not be diagnosed as educational but is basically medical or psychiatric. The piece of information, critical in the diagnosis, which may be withheld by the girl from a middle-class truant officer, is less likely to be concealed from a social peer. Add to the above functions the increasing thrust towards self-determination by minority groups, and one easily sees why "new careers" has assumed the character and organizational trappings of a movement, and has gained adherents rapidly.

Apart from the politization of its leadership, "new careers" contains the germ of a synergistic solution to several convergent problems for the poor but, as presently structured, has inherent problems of its own. Although a new, connective link, previously absent in poverty areas, is forged, and although a middle-range pool of semiskilled manpower is created where professional services are scarce, training community workers in "new careers" is by no means the single solution to the paucity and fragmentation of professional services for the poor. Yet, with modifications, it can be viewed as a seminal concept.

The word "career" suggests both the source of some of the difficulties and the way to resolve them. Most of the new community jobs have been created and funded by federal fiat. Many have proven to be low paid, entry-level jobs and not the bottom rungs of a career ladder, with opportunities for further training and promotion. For example, there were approximately 3,000 teacher aides working in Chicago schools in 1969. Few had opportunities for further education and, only after two years, were plans developed to include them in the civil service merit system.[a] Nationwide, there are about 400,000 nurses aides and 96,000 psychiatric aides, and few are offered opportunities for further training, while all hospital workers, especially women, are notoriously underpaid.

Strikes, sit-ins and protests by new careerists began to erupt in eastern cities in 1970 as participants correctly perceived that their jobs were the end, as well as the beginning, of opportunity. With the cutbacks in federal poverty programs, some of the jobs were totally wiped out, and it remains to be seen what will happen to others as college graduates pour into a slack job market in increasing numbers. Another fundamental difficulty is to be found in the uneasy truce that prevails in some offices, clinics or classrooms, between professional workers and their new assistants because their respective responsibilities and strengths were often left unclarified.

The community colleges, burgeoning during the same period, have become increasingly interested in collaborative training programs for new, middle-range, human service and public service occupations. A 1970 survey of college programs for paraprofessionals found nearly 20,000 students at 160 institutions. A far from inclusive survey, it was limited to only the most structured of programs, focusing exclusively on degree-granting programs for full-time employees of human service agencies, who had been given time off with pay to attend school.[2]

The direct involvement of professional schools and universities, however, with few exceptions, has been scattered and exceedingly limited. But it is here that the most profound and perplexing educational issues are to be found. The lack of opportunities for occupational mobility within some of the professions, notably medicine and the allied health professions, has become an increasingly troublesome issue as growing standardization and inflexibility of educational and certification requirements block paths of entry and flow within professional fields.

Yet if a career ladder that leads from entry level jobs to professional ones is to be fully articulated, the involvement of senior institutions is essential. Thus,

---

[a]In the New York City public school system, some categories of paraprofessionals were brought into the civil service system earlier, and funds were appropriated in 1971 expressly for their educational training programs. In Chicago, however, budgetary cutbacks in 1971 reduced the program.

for example, if a child-care assistant working in a day-care center, who studied initially at a community college, is to have the opportunity to become a certified teacher, by working and studying in combination or alternatively, the senior institutions alone hold access to the upper rungs of the professional ladder.

Unless career ladders and lattices are clearly defined, based on a careful analysis of the tasks to be performed, and then built into the structure of the professions and into the merit system of civil service, the new community programs emerge as little more than stop-gap, unemployment expediencies. Without disparaging the vital need for short-term measures to relieve acute unemployment, it would be unfortunate to lose sight of chronic problems, of the longer-range possibilities for rationalizing the delivery of human services, and of providing new avenues for community and personal development. In pursuing these further objectives, the participation of universities and colleges is required.

Fundamental changes in professional practices and education are implicit in fulfilling the above objectives, but they are, as yet, largely unacknowledged. Programmatically, this is obviously no small task. Workable programs require the cooperation of the three, principal pace-setters in each profession, all resistant to change, namely: (1) the educational institutions that offer training; (2) the professional societies or state boards that define standards of performance through licensure, accreditation and certification; and (3) the major employers, whether they be public agencies such as school boards or civil service commissions or private institutions such as hospitals.

Reform in professional practices is long overdue, and the models designed to resolve acute problems in poverty areas may have wide applicability elsewhere. Institutions of higher education can participate in this complex task in several ways, each reinforcing the other, and some already underway.

Education and Training

Although institutions of higher education stand somewhat outside the invidious circle, described earlier, of limited opportunity and deficient community services in poverty areas, they are deeply implicated as educators. This is a key role, one that is obvious and universally acknowledged.

Colleges and universities provide the education required to enter professions at middle and upper echelons of responsibility across the gamut of fields. They educate doctors and nurses, teachers and principals, lawyers, engineers, accountants, planners, social workers, economists and psychologists. They now train a variety of technicians, auxiliary personnel, and paraprofessionals, as well, in the community colleges. Furthermore, they educate the faculty that teaches the future teachers, social workers, technicians and paraprofessionals.

In recruitment and admission policies and in academic requirements, they are thus, first and foremost, the gatekeepers for entry into professional fields and for professional advancement, largely by screening out the unqualified. Second, the faculties of colleges and universities also determine the contents, scope and style of professional education.

The chief and virtually exclusive route of entry into most professions today is formal college attendance, which would have prevented Abraham Lincoln from practicing law or shut out Frank Lloyd Wright from architecture or Jane Addams from being a social worker. The absence of alternative paths of entry and of full-blown career ladders within the professions is an apparent response to the growth of professional knowledge and complex techniques, with the consequent necessity to assure standards of competence. But might it not also be a partial response to the pecking order within a profession, a semiartifice to maintain semimonopolistic positions, so as to make it unthinkable for a nurse, however competent, to aspire to become a physician?

To counteract the narrow social horizons and one-dimensional stratification prevailing in some professions, there has been a movement, most recently, to "screen-in" students, previously barred from entering into professions, by actively recruiting and assisting poor and minority students in professional schools as well as in community colleges. These efforts have produced a substantial increase in the number of minority students in professional schools, notably Blacks.[b] But virtually unsurmountable age, race, sex and other socioeconomic status barriers still persist. An effort is also underway to update curricula and pedagogical methods to meet contemporary urban needs in many fields as, for example, the revised and compressed time span in the education of physicians or programs to better prepare future teachers for inner-city schools.

Specific ways of refurbishing educational elements and of carving fresh paths of access, differ considerably in each field. For example, the clinical model, the close association of practice and precept that characterizes medical education, has wide applicability elsewhere, especially in teaching, social work, and public administration, where internships and field work are often much less satisfactory. Several leading law schools have strengthened their clinical programs in the last two years. Yet, in medicine itself, the involvement of practicing physicians in most phases of medical education has been an exceedingly conservative force, acting to restrain innovation, new curriculum designs, and new perceptions of medical roles. A number of issues, however, cut across several professional fields.

---

[b]The preliminary, as yet unpublished, tabulations of the Office of Civil Rights (HEW) revealed that in three, graduate professional fields, the percentages of minority students enrolled in 1970 were as follows:

	Total No. of Students	Negro (Percent)	Hispanic-American (Percent)	Oriental (Percent)	American-Indian (Percent)
Medicine	43,958	4.2	0.8	1.8	0.1
Law	64,871	3.9	1.1	0.5	0.3
Dentistry	16,737	3.6	0.8	1.8	0.1

Manpower shortages exist in uneven degrees within special sectors of each profession, by far the greatest in the health professions and the least in teaching, where an oversupply is projected in all but a few specialized fields. By enlarging, streamlining and redirecting their present programs to meet anticipated demands for personnel in short supply, professional schools could make a significant contribution to easing manpower shortages and thereby presumably help the poor, who are at the margins of service. Since the aggregate capacities for graduate and professional education in several areas far exceed expected future needs, a correction of these imbalances, painful as it may be, is essential for the sake of the student and to maximize scarce institutional resources.[3] An increase in the total supply of professional and technical workers in tight labor markets would presumably trickle more services down to the poor.

Simply training more men and women, even of more heterogenous backgrounds, to fill existing roles, however, will only partially alleviate the pressures for services in poverty areas. Medicine offers the best example of this for there is virtually no way to catch up in the next decade with the acute shortage of physicians or to meet the health care needs of the nation, much less of the poor, without a major overhaul of the health-care system itself. Even if medical training facilities were doubled immediately, even if financial hurdles were overcome and comprehensive payment or prepayment plans were enacted tomorrow, a more effective system for delivering services and utilizing personnel efficiently is still required.[4] Otherwise, reducing the financial impediments to health care would serve mostly to augment effective demand. It would refuel the already sky-rocketing costs of health care and highlight the weaknesses in the present system.

The National Academy of Science, for example, recently proposed a health-team approach to meet the problem with the establishment of three new classes of physician helpers. What they proposed, in essence, was the creation of new professional roles and a new career ladder.[5] Prior to that proposal, a number of universities had already inaugurated programs to train new types of health personnel.[c] Altogether, about 100 such programs are in existence, with approximately another 100 in the planning stage. They exemplify but one of the numerous ways to facilitate the delivery of health care that are suggested or already in operation, all requiring the active participation of institutions of higher educa-

[c]Duke University was one of the first to introduce, in 1965, the Physician's Assistant Program (now called Physician's Associate Program). The program was aimed primarily at training returning Health Corps servicemen to perform a range of civilian medical tasks under the supervision of practicing physicians. A similar program, called MEDEX, was initiated in 1969 at the University of Washington. In pediatrics, the University of Colorado Medical Center has pioneered since 1965 in the training of Pediatric Nurse Practitioners. The latter, after completing a baccalaureate RN degree, are given four additional months' training which qualifies them to assume many of the pediatrician's duties in connection with caring for healthy children or simple illnesses. The University of Colorado has also developed another short pediatric training sequence called Child Health Associate, which is designed for high school graduates.

tion if they are to succeed and all raising thorny, unresolved questions with regard to accreditation, certification and accountability.

Systemic Reform

While internal educational adaptation may be the first order of business, it is evident that revisions in professional education of the scale and depth required to address the problems of the poor cannot be undertaken by institutions of higher learning in isolation. One of the real bottlenecks in improving and updating professional education, best exemplified perhaps in schools of education, is that the curricula of the professional schools must respond to certification standards set outside the schools. The training offered students obviously must be in phase with certification criteria and actual employment opportunities for graduates. Consequently, the levers for comprehensive change, internally as well as in the communities of the poor, are to be found off-campus in the very structure of the professions.

A second responsibility, therefore, rests implicitly with institutions of higher education. As partners with fellow practitioners, they can point the way to basic reforms with remodeled modes for rendering professional services. Alternatively, they could choose to hang back as bystanders, and thus accomplices, to prevailing inequities and inefficiencies.

To inaugurate a legal aid bureau for the poor, for example, is relatively easy and certainly useful. Nor is it difficult to train local residents as legal assistants, competent to advise on many of the domestic difficulties, consumer fraud and credit issues, the imponderable byways of the public bureaucracies, or rental and leasing problems that typify the practice of poverty law. But legal assistants have no standing in the profession; indeed they are vulnerable to indictment for practicing without a license. Whether a viable, middle-range, semiskilled occupational role can or should be defined is a question that can be explored expeditiously by a law school faculty. Columbia University Law School and several others have already embarked on such training programs or have cooperated with community colleges in their design, and the Association of American Law Schools is preparing a detailed proposal for a one-year course of training for adult paraprofessionals.[6] Yet, beyond such proposals and the other forms of involvement with class action suits in poverty areas, a deeper contribution to the legal problems of the poor is to be made by focusing faculty and student attention upon the laws themselves, on the nature of leaseholds in the slum, on the unequal status of landlord and tenant before the bar, or similarly, on the criminal code, on garnishment statutes, or upon the deficiencies in the judicial system itself.

To draw another illustration from the field of teaching, there is considerable dissatisfaction throughout the nation with the ways in which teachers are educated, accredited and appointed. At the heart of several proposed reforms is the belief that the permanent certification of teachers and the selection of supervisors should not be based solely on college credits or formal examinations. Minority groups believe that these procedures have been discriminatory, and school supervisors suggest that they are overly standardized and sterile so that talented teachers are often barred from accreditation while grossly inadequate teachers regularly receive it. Instead of the present system, a carefully supervised internship period, of perhaps three to five years, might be instituted prior to certification. Much of the actual teacher training would then be shifted from college campuses into school classrooms.[7]

A specific variant of this approach was proposed in 1970 for the schools in the nation's capital. The public school system in Washington, D.C., whose students are 94.8% black, has undertaken a massive effort to teach children to read.[8] In consultation with the Metropolitan Applied Research Center directed by Kenneth B. Clark, a noted black educator and psychologist, a comprehensive plan was devised to improve the teaching of reading. Its distinguishing feature was a new system of professional advancement that was linked either to the demonstrated ability of teachers to raise the educational achievement of their pupils or to the help they rendered other developing teachers in the system. Instead of paying teachers according to length of service and college degrees, the prevailing modes, the new pay-scale was patterned after the collegiate system of promotion. The beginning teacher would work under supervision for the first three years, much like the medical intern or resident. If qualified, he or she would then be certified at a rank comparable to an assistant professor in a university. The next grades in the hierarchy would be senior teachers and, finally, master teachers, the equivalent of a full professor, to be paid at least as much as a principal. Thus, teachers of demonstrated ability might receive top salaries without becoming administrators. In essence, what was proposed to raise pupil achievement in Washington, D.C., was a fundamental revision of established practices and professional roles. That the proposal encountered fierce resistance from the teachers' union and other established educational organizations is scarcely surprising.[d]

The public school system in Chicago and in all large cities has been no more successful in teaching black, inner-city children than in Washington, D.C. Yet, one-third of the principals in Chicago's schools in 1969 had worked at their assigned schools for less than a year; their salary scales were tied to school size so that to be promoted or get a raise, a good principal had to be transferred to a larger school. One-third of the teachers manning the classrooms in Chicago schools were full-time, uncertified substitute teachers and had been so for some time. Clearly, there is little prospect for building a creative esprit within a school or effective teaching teams without addressing some of these basic staffing practices.

---

[d]The original plan was somewhat modified since the local teacher's union particularly objected to an initial proposal to link salary scales to pupil performance on periodically administered, achievement tests.

Clearly, universities are singularly well-equipped and well-placed to look beyond their walls, to identify the roadblocks to professional and institutional reform, to formulate alternative ways of proceeding, and to precipitate a process of change. Experimental programs that can be undertaken internally as, for example, follow-up seminars for graduates in the first critical year of teaching or new kinds of training for indigenous teacher aides and auxiliary personnel, are not to be minimized. Rather, it is to emphasize a deeper, more extensive involvement in professional and institutional change. The vast majority of Illinois public school teachers, for example, were educated in its public colleges and universities. The system itself, as well as the stream of new entrants, is the direct concern of educators in public universities.

Traditionally, the faculties of professional schools have led the movement for reform in professional practice, despite the strains necessarily entailed, often a few paces ahead of the practitioner, but not so far ahead as to lose contact and influence. Unless they assume this role vis-a-vis the poor, educators will find themselves turning out technicians to fill existing job slots, rather than professionals with a vision of what their role ought to be.

Human Services in Public Agencies

The chief instruments for widely dispersed transformations in the services rendered the poor are in the hands of public agencies, particularly state agencies, who, by law, bear residual responsibility for health, education, welfare, corrections, and the like. State colleges and universities have a singular opportunity to work with their sister agencies in state government to bring about significant improvements in the gamut of public services.

State and local governments are the major employers of professional and auxiliary personnel in human service fields. Over 75% of the jobs in social welfare and human service fields, open to persons with a bachelor's degree or less, in Illinois for example, are to be found in government.[9] Twice as many persons, without a bachelor's degree, in human service occupations work for governmental agencies than for private agencies. The proportion is reversed for professionals, holding, for example, a master's degree in social work, who are more often employed by private, voluntary agencies. Four-fifths of all accredited social workers are engaged in individual and family casework. The opportunity to improve human services on a mass basis is to be found only in public agencies—largely state agencies.

A collaborative effort to rationalize state public service employment, matched with revised curricula in state colleges and universities is entirely feasible. In fact, it has already begun to happen in isolated instances in several states, including Illinois. The Public Service Institute at the Loop College of the City Colleges of Chicago, for example, has been working closely with local authorities in city, county and state agencies for some years now, offering in-service training programs for their employees on released, agency time. New systems for delivering services with linkages at the community-area level, newly defined occupational roles and career opportunities in public service can and are being devised, and educational offerings must be synchronized. Large-scale and immediate pay-offs, both in improving the quality of services for the poor and in opening opportunities for employment at entry level jobs and for promotion, are to be found in the reform of public agency personnel practices.

The Human Service Manpower Career Center of the Illinois Department of Labor, for example, was established "to stimulate and support the recruitment, training and utilization of new manpower through inter-agency planning, research and project development."[10] Under its aegis and in collaboration with the Illinois Department of Personnel, a new career ladder for the Department of Mental Health was devised and tested in the field. It has since been approved by the Illinois Civil Service Commission. A similar manpower and job analysis was completed in the field of adult corrections. The new personnel system of the Department of Mental Health incorporates several features essential to an effective career ladder.

1. It provides the Department with entry level openings for new workers at every educational level from high school equivalency (rather than high school completion) through the master's degree;

2. It makes possible for incumbent employees to move upward from within on the basis of successful completion of in-service training, work experience and job performance, rather than only through formal academic training;

3. It sets up a sequence of four in-service training sets to enable workers to obtain the necessary preparation for career advancement at various steps in the ladder; and

4. The series expresses the generalist concept throughout, allowing for broad flexibility in its application and considerable horizontal mobility of workers.[11]

The unrealized potential for productive interaction and synchronized efforts between state agencies and state colleges in human and public service fields is enormous.[e] The responsibilities of many state agencies and the educational and research concerns of faculty in state colleges and universities are often parallel. Comparable opportunities exist for collaborative research and training programs with municipal governments.[f]

---

[e]Numerous examples of potentially significant areas for collaborative collegiate efforts with Illinois state governmental agencies can be cited: the Department of Local Government Affairs, in truly comprehensive regional and urban planning; the Department of Business and Economic Development, in community economic development corporations or minority businesses; the Governor's Office of Human Resources or the Division of Vocational and Technical Education, in manpower training to name but a few.

[f]For example, the *New York Times*, 12 July 1971, reported that as a result of the major controversy provoked by the costly proliferation of management and consultant studies in

In sum, if colleges and universities limit their horizons in revising professional education and curricula to what can be accomplished internally, reflecting standards and requirements determined by others, their spheres of action and potential effectiveness will be relatively narrow. State and local government are the natural staging area for testing new kinds of coordinate programs developed in the state system of higher education.

Community Projects

The point of departure for innovations and for appraising their effectiveness as well, is to be found in the projects organized by community groups in conjunction with institutions of higher education. The child-care center described in Appendix C, the community health center, the storefront academy, workshop and clinic provide a setting not only for service, but for fresh ways of perceiving and evaluating professional activities. The wellsprings of new ideas, pragmatic solutions, and proving grounds are in neighborhood-based, autonomous, client-oriented projects.

New linkages among professional services will be forged at the community level quite naturally if self-determination and self-help characterize their organization. New semiprofessional roles for community outreach and intake personnel, whose skills bridge several fields, will emerge. Although a particular project may be geared initially to a single objective such as a health-care center or an economic development corporation, other collateral projects and programs will soon evolve spontaneously, of necessity, to enhance its efficacy. And perhaps more effective structures for interrelating functional programs will emerge as well.

The community development projects that have been most successful in various parts of the country have typically started out with a single concrete objective, which then became the central star in a constellation of related programs. For example, in one of the poorest counties of the nation and of Mississippi, the school of medicine of Tufts University organized a community health center in 1965, with funds from the Office of Economic Opportunity. Although the center dispensed health care and served patients daily, its purpose soon became much more comprehensive. Health care proved to be just one of the services of the center. Food, jobs, education, housing, sanitation, water, care for the elderly, and a host of other new programs were spun off from the original one. A public bus service and a cooperative marketing agency were organized. In a county so poor that even hope was a luxury, aspirations and an active determina-

New York City, an urban analysis center was created at City University of New York in 1971. An initial appropriation of one million dollars was allocated to City University and another half million dollars set aside for research and consultative studies in private universities.[12] In Chapter 11, the creation of a statewide Institute for Social Policy is proposed as one of the ways to elicit collaborative programs.

tion to improve living conditions were rekindled by the presence of the center. In short, important social, economic and political changes were underway.[g]

The point of entry into the cycle of poverty was a health-care center, but it was soon obvious that to treat cases of rat bites or lead poisoning daily and then to send the patient back to squalid housing was running a treadmill. Nor could nutrition be much improved without raising incomes; it was evident that education and job training were just as significant to improving health as innoculations.[14]

If the point of entry into the cycle of poverty were instead an economic development corporation, a manpower training program, a project to raise educational achievement in schools or to reduce delinquency and crime, a health center would surely need to be established. Thus, from the standpoint of higher education, the particular project or its initial focus and objective is far less important than that it be structured in such a way as to respond to the pragmatic needs of community groups. Then the project is far more likely to bring about real changes in neighborhood living conditions and, only then, will it be truly oriented toward discovery. For experts and consultants to prescribe, a priori, the organizational structure and objectives of a project in a poverty area is to limit, in advance, its potential usefulness as a field experiment. Yet for institutions of higher learning, community projects are ideal vehicles for devising and testing alternative instruments for delivering services and educating students.

Of course, the professional school or faculty, let us say a college of medicine, that cooperates with a community group in the establishment of a new project may have neither competence nor interest in the correlated satellite projects that might evolve, such as projects to improve housing or sanitation. The medical school might nevertheless serve as a bridge to other departments or colleges, as for example, the college of engineering or architecture or urban planning.

What is envisioned ultimately in the communities of the poor are nuclear projects that will attract satellite projects and expand to engage the participation of several professional schools, disciplines, or even at times, several institutions. The educational and research benefits to be derived from the cross-fertilization of faculty and students in diverse fields, working in tandem to achieve joint objectives, are potentially very great. Autonomous community projects can be one of the ways to span the chasm between professional schools and other parts of the university.

---

[g]Despite these many tangible benefits, the Center was closed in 1971 for lack of funds, a victim of the economic recession and public parsimony. The parallel urban health center also established by Tufts in a poverty area of Boston, had met with somewhat less success for a variety of reasons. Among them was the manner in which it was organized and controlled. Since the urban health center was not autonomous of the university, it had been a very costly drain on university resources and a point of controversy (encountering staffing problems as well).[13]

Evaluation and Collaborative Research

University faculty, particularly in the social sciences, often have highly developed critical and analytic skills, which have been cultivated in their education and work and which can be exceedingly valuable in appraising community projects. If the experience gained in prototypical projects is to be recycled in a useful manner, critical evaluation of innovations is essential. Only then, when judged in terms of their actual effects on the target groups who sponsor them, can they be refined on the basis of empirical evidence and feedback information for improving educational programs as well.

New techniques of policy analysis emerging in the social sciences have direct application to community development projects. Analytic techniques successfully used in industry and defense to clarify complex decision-making, such as cost-benefit or cost-effectiveness studies, systems analysis, program budgeting and network analysis have potential applicability to a host of social and public programs.

Paradoxically, the stance of the systems analyst and that of the neighborhood target group is curiously consonant. Both tend to focus on concrete objectives and results, while for both the means of achieving a defined objective are the variables. Both consciously recognize and are sensitive to the interconnectedness of disparate programs and to the secondary, as well as the direct, consequences of events.

In contrast, practitioners and large public agencies tend to be caught up with and locked into established ways of delivering services. Indeed, it is their express responsibility. Thus, they are quite naturally preoccupied with means, or inputs, instead of ends, the outputs or effects of their activities. One has only to look at the corpus of social statistics generated by public agencies to illustrate the point. A vast body of data is collected about costs, facilities and expenditures of programs, in essence, their inputs. In contrast, relatively few data are collected about the results of these activities, their outputs, whether they be the immediate results of particular programs or their wider, secondary social effects.

In the case of education, for example, volumes of statistics enumerate teachers, institutions, facilities, student attendance, cost and expenditures, in essence, inputs into the educational system. Some data on program results or outputs are also available, usually measured by the number of graduates or by educational attainment levels. But only recently have serious efforts been undertaken to measure systematically and precisely educational outputs, for example, what pupils actually learn.[h]

---

[h]The best example of recent endeavors to measure educational outputs is the National Assessment of Educational Progress. The project which has federal and foundation support is being conducted under the auspices of Education Commission of the States, an organiza-

If self-help and self-determination characterize the organization of community projects, the focus will necessarily shift from the professional dispensers of services to their consumers and thereby from program inputs to program outcomes. The success of a project, let us say a storefront tutoring project, is generally judged by its local sponsors in terms of its noticeable effects on the participants. Some results may be measurable, as for example, improved performance by pupils in standard achievement tests or in higher grades at school. Others may not be quantified so easily, such as attitudinal changes, increased self-esteem, self-confidence, perseverance, creativity, or self-discipline. Tangible results are also both direct and indirect. For example, if the tutors were junior high school students and the tutees first graders, it might be found that the immediate, measurable improvement in school achievement would be greater for the tutors than for the tutees.[i] Or, perhaps the renewed progress and interest of her children in education might stir the mother or others in the family to seek further education themselves.

This sort of simple common-sense focus on objectives and results regularly gets obscured in large-scale public programs as they filter through the administrative complexities of massive bureaucracies, which, of course, have come to have a life and purpose of their own. The stance of the scientist and of some social scientists is eminently empirical and pragmatic, and so, of necessity, is that of the poor. Thus, there is a nice congruence of viewpoints about social programs and a genuine opportunity to explore and jointly to perfect new techniques of policy analysis and evaluation.

The analytic and critical skills residing in faculty of various departments of a university can be drawn together to yield interdisciplinary insights in a new way. These capacities can be exceedingly useful in separating those new approaches that are viable and effective from those that are counterproductive or dilatory. After all, novelty is not the same as discovery, and even though creative innovation is most needed, bad ideas and failures are to be anticipated as well as good ones. Social programs with yardsticks formulated in advance for evaluating results are exceptional, and this is something that might distinguish collaborative university-community projects. Although social scientists, scientists, and educators have no nostrums for urban ills and no ready answers for the questions that they raise, they do have ways of proceeding and perceiving that might be extraordinarily valuable in developing and appraising new ventures and new ideas.

---

tion of state officials and educators. The research design and much of the work is under the supervision of Dr. Ralph W. Tyler, a prominent behavioral scientist and educator. A sample of over 100,000 students and adults in various regions of the country was tested in 10 subject areas to find out what they actually knew. The results of the test in two of the subject areas were released in July 1970. The tests will be repeated with similarly large regional samples at periodic intervals in the future.

[i]This has occurred frequently in tutoring programs, which have proven to be of great benefit to the tutors themselves.[15]

In summary, the most desirable service programs for the urban poor are those in which the concerns of a community group and the interests of faculty and students are complementary. When mutual benefits are anticipated, the relationship of a college and a community group can be similar to that of any professional and his client. Even though no fee for services may be involved in the transaction, the relationship would be essentially contractual through an exchange of nonmonetary benefits. This kind of symbiotic relationship in service projects contrasts with one in which services are extended by experts, magnanimously, in the spirit of noblesse oblige. It is likely to be more dignified, effective and viable.

To achieve a working relationship, however, requires deliberate effort on the part of the college and a sustained commitment over time of both personnel and funds. Prior to any of this, the university or college must take the initiative to dispel the natural distrust or outright hostility provoked by its sheer physical presence and seemingly foreign and arcane ways. Working backwards, let us now look at the college or university as an institutional presence in a neighborhood and consider the milieu in which community projects for the poor might take root and flourish.

10 The Campus and the Climate of Cooperation

Town-gown relations have troubled universities since the Middle Ages. Since institutions of higher education have been grappling with these problems for centuries, the more general issues will not be addressed here. With regard to building satisfactory working relationships with the urban poor and with minority groups, however, there are a few contemporary wrinkles.

A college or university is a formidable institutional presence in any town or neighborhood, especially a poor one. As such, it can be a powerful force for widening opportunity and improving the quality of neighborhood life or instead it can engender fierce resentments. Often the urban college or university and the urban slum are proximate in space, but they may be otherwise miles apart. Because of its social distance and its physical proximity, sometimes attenuated by differences in race as well, the college or university must consciously seek ways to become a valuable and trusted local institution if it is to live in harmony with its neighbors.

Every institution has neighborhood and regional functions, even if it serves statewide, often worldwide, constituencies. But some colleges, particularly community colleges or rural state colleges, define their chief mission locally. Even when a college is physically removed from densely concentrated areas of poverty, if it is to offer students and faculty educational and research experiences that equip them to function in contemporary urban society, it also has an obligation to reach out to the poor. The community college, of course, should be a part of and belong to its community. When it happens to be situated in a poverty area, it has the greatest opportunity to be responsive to local needs. Whatever its geographic situation, its size or mission, each institution in a state system shares the responsibility for developing vehicles of communication with the urban poor.

Channels of Communication

An open, two-way flow of communication is the initial aim so that the intersecting interests of an institution and a community group can be identified (as well as the points of grievance before they become incendiary). The particular channels for achieving this flow will vary with the nature of the institution and of the community. Many colleges and universities have designated specific officers to be responsible for neighborhood relations. Whatever its form, the involvement of an institution in local affairs requires a parallel internal structure. The spokesman of the institution must be sufficiently knowledgeable, empathic and canny to sort out the representations of responsible interest groups from irresponsible demands and to fend off veiled threats. He must be invested with sufficient authority to negotiate from strength in order to respond in reality to legitimate proposals, to avoid entanglements in internecine leadership struggles by rival groups, and to preserve the flexibility, autonomy and interests of the institution.

Explicit, defined vehicles for liaison are important since they provide a definite place where local citizens can make initial contact with the college and through which faculty can become acquainted with various sectors and interest groups in the community. In poverty areas, an identifiable office where citizens can come in person and be assured of an attentive hearing with a follow-up is usually desirable. It is preferably located somewhere on a ground floor where it may easily be approached without traversing the entire campus. On a large university campus, such an office could serve as a clearinghouse or information bureau, and its personnel would include people from the neighborhood. As suggested earlier, if an institution of higher education did nothing more than offer community groups practical assistance in threading their way through the maze of existing public and private programs for the poor, they would be performing a singularly useful function. A college is also a good link with the local business community. These liaison and consultative activities with faculty, government, business and voluntary agencies can be a prime function of a neighborhood relations office.

Numerous universities and senior colleges have also established outposts in poverty areas, at some distance from their campuses.[a] Once a cooperative service project in a poverty area has been established as for example, the educational opportunity outposts proposed earlier, it, too, can serve as a bridge to other divisions of the college. Some community colleges have organized local citizens advisory boards with whom to consult about particular programs. Until recently, however, such boards have predominantly represented the business and professional community. Their composition might be enlarged to encompass other social sectors in the region, or special advisory boards might be created for projects in depressed areas. Whatever the vehicle most appropriate to the structure and geographic location of an institution, it should clearly express the message of Welcome—not just to the person or group but to his views and problems.

More important in the long run for establishing a climate of cooperation and trust than any administrative device is the observed behavior of the institution in the community. Only its actions and actual policies will lend credence to the rhetoric of cooperation. When, for example, the University of Illinois lent its

---

[a]As for example, the projects in East St. Louis staffed by faculty and students of the Edwardsville campus of Southern Illinois University or the Center for Inner City Studies of Northeastern Illinois State College.

its support and technical assistance to desegregating the public schools in Champaign-Urbana, this act expressed its policies to the local community far better than any neighborhood or public relations office could.

Corporate Activities

Colleges and universities are large institutions and necessarily engaged in many corporate and entrepreneurial activities as well as educational ones. All large institutions hire and fire workers, construct buildings, purchase supplies, and create housing, traffic, police, and parking problems. These kinds of transactions offer additional pragmatic ways to build a climate of cooperation in a poverty neighborhood. They can be a part of the connective tissue of good communication and a prelude to mutually beneficial endeavors.

It would seem unnecessary to emphasize that a college or university should be a model employer and that all forms of overt discrimination in employment on the basis of race, religion, ethnicity or sex be promptly rooted out. Veiled discrimination, however, does persist in corners of any large institution. While it is difficult to override the personal preferences or prejudices of faculty, it is the responsibility of the administration to see that particular laboratories and departmental offices that consistently appear to discriminate and never hire minority employees alter their practices.

In addition, within their own institution, administrators can take a more aggressive stance to promote job opportunities for the poor by recruiting neighborhood workers and devising appropriate training programs. Career ladders and in-service education can be offered to present employees so that opportunities for promotion as well as entry-level jobs are provided to local citizens. Harvard University, for example, launched such a program in 1970, supported by funds from the Department of Labor; it also included English language instruction for Spanish-American employees and several additional summer employment projects for Cambridge youths.[1]

Other avenues for building a climate of cooperation and for actively combating latent discrimination are to be found in the construction, maintenance and procurement activities of the institution. Construction companies, for example, engaged by colleges (in fact any company with whom they do business) should be expected to give evidence of a desegregated work force. When this is not the case, as is likely with large construction companies where discriminatory practices have prevailed for decades, the employment of minority subcontractors can be required. To cite another example at Harvard University, a special committee was established in 1969, charged with the task of devising a formula to increase minority workers on university construction projects at every level of skill. As a result of the committee's work, specific manning tables, under which contractors guaranteed to hire minority workers, were included in all university contracts.

Subcontracts were also awarded to minority firms, and a special officer has been employed to monitor compliance with these policies.[2]

In addition to construction projects, procurement is another institutional activity with local leverages. Faculty or administrative personnel can consult with fledgling local entrepreneurs or help in organizing a community economic development corporation in poverty areas. The latter can be encouraged to compete for contracts to supply some of the many products and services regularly and routinely purchased by large institutions, for such things as food service, repair services, paper and office supplies. When necessary, arbitrary impediments should be eliminated so that new entrepreneurs may be informed of and can comply with the procurement standards of the college.

Physical Presence

Apart from its corporate and entrepreneurial operations, the college or university is also a dominant and sometimes a forbidding physical presence in a neighborhood. It is usually one with enviable facilities and often one with acute space needs for expansion.

The situation of the community college with regard to these matters is somewhat different from that of a large senior institution, even a commuter university. Since the community college serves a limited territory with a much smaller, defined constituency, everywhere but in large metropolitan regions, it is an arm of the community area and should thoroughly reflect the taste, style and priorities of its constituency. The latter may be quite heterogeneous, socially and economically, even in small- and medium-sized cities and surely in the outlying suburban towns of major cities. In the suburban ring, despite residential segregation, poor and rich, black and white, and Spanish-Americans often live in adjacent townships and neighborhoods. Consequently, a deliberate effort must be made to assure that the interests of each of the varied sectors of the region are actually reflected in the activities of the college.

The community college, with its doors open round-the-clock and round-the-calendar, is the nearest approximation to a community center in numerous sprawling, urbanized areas. When located in an economically depressed area, it is a bridge between the greater society and the isolated poor. The absence of a sense of community, of identity, and of place is as prevalent in some of the new suburban accretions as in the inner city. The community college, in its formal and informal courses, cultural activities, meeting rooms, libraries and sport facilities, in essence performs the same function whether in city, suburb or hinterland. Ideally, it can serve as an agent of community cohesiveness, sociability, communication, culture, recreation, opportunity; in poverty areas, it can be a catalyst for social and economic development.

In rural areas, many of which are losing population for lack of employment opportunities, the community college performs a vital function in equipping youths and adult workers, whose skills are obsolete, with new transferable, employable skills. Cooperative, agricultural extension programs of land-grant universities and other community development projects of state universities have been of great assistance in depressed rural areas. But few, similarly excellent and effective services are made available to the urban poor, relative to their numbers.

The community colleges which happen to be located near concentrated centers of urban poverty can become the chief avenues for social and economic development. The colleges already do attempt to serve the many talented individuals from low-income families, motivated to move upward and outward, by providing remedial, occupational and transfer programs and by reinforcing aspirations with realistic opportunities for socially useful and personally rewarding achievement. Such community colleges, however, can also provide the geographic focal point for concrete and practical programs for overall community development of the kind suggested earlier.

Those colleges located in or near urban poverty areas should be encouraged to work with local groups and institutions in developing their curricula and in setting up model demonstration centers, built around pragmatic neighborhood problems. These new centers would be designed to supply services needed in the neighborhood in connection with the college's educational programs. Technical and vocational educational curricula can be expanded in conjunction with the newly established centers as, for example, restaurant, food handling and nutrition centers; or centers for early education; or small business administration, legal and commercial service centers; or comprehensive health and infant welfare centers.

The college would offer the tools for community development, library and research facilities, the technical assistance of its faculty, appropriate formal course work, and part-time staff from its student apprentices enrolled in work-study programs. The faculties of the college would draw on the consultative resources of the university and senior colleges and, when necessary, draw them in directly. Vocational education in some fields is more appropriately offered in conjunction with on-the-job training in local businesses or at the high school level. Linkages with local high schools can be strengthened by making college faculty available as curricula consultants or by permitting high school students to register for a particular course when given only at the college.

A plurality of highly diverse, open institutions, with arms reaching out to a variety of appended local projects, is envisioned. As the focal point of community development, the colleges become a window to the world for isolated community groups. They provide a pleasant setting for recreation, culture, and sociability otherwise lacking in poverty areas. Comfortable, lively and attractive places, open summers, weekends and evenings, they can be places of promise, where effort is rewarded with tangible personal and community benefits. They can become islands of prodigious opportunity in a sea of unrelieved frustration.

Senior institutions and universities, of course, serve a constituency with a broader territorial base than the community college, and their activities cannot be as intimately linked with a defined community area. But they can be no less responsive to the needs of their neighbors, including nearby sister educational institutions.

Many of the activities described above might equally well occur in a senior college. State colleges and universities often offer organized summer sport and recreational programs for neighborhood youth as well as upward bound and college prep programs. Book stores, meeting rooms, counseling and testing services and the like, if possible, should be made available to neighbors. They should be welcome at public functions, lectures and cultural events. Even if the public is invited, however, only a limited number of events are likely to attract neighbors since most are geared to the interests of students and faculty. Some programs, such as political speakers, local leaders, well-known rock bands, or local art fairs and exhibits, have very wide appeal and should be deliberately scheduled annually, so that the campus itself is not perceived as a hostile and isolated island. Instead, it should be viewed as a place to which neighbors can comfortably repair for technical and professional advice in community development projects and a place where they can expect to be received with respect.

The most contentious issue, in recent years, between higher education and the poor relates to the physical expansion plans of colleges or univerities and to questions of turf or territoriality. One recalls, for example, that the plans to locate the New Jersey College of Medicine in Newark touched off the riots of 1967 and set the city ablaze, or to cite another example, the ill-fated initial plans for a gymnasium at Columbia University and the subsequent student disorders. Far less dramatically, however, the expansion of colleges, hospitals, and other large institutions in the inner city has been virtually called to a halt by organized protests of community groups in many cities. The experience of Boston University, Temple University, the University of Pennsylvania, and other urban universities has been essentially similar, even though violent confrontations may have been obviated. Until the shortage of low and medium-income housing is alleviated or unless sufficient relocation housing is made available, it can be assumed that major institutional expansion through massive slum clearance has been effectively foreclosed in the immediate future.

When a senior college or university is located near an acutely depressed poverty area, it stands in glittering contrast to its surroundings, but the problems of its neighbors often spill onto its campus. Such colleges have a Hobson's Choice of building a fortress campus or creating an ambiance that is compatible with both the needs of the community and the institution. The President of Columbia University, Dr. William J. McGill, expressed the latter aim succinctly.

The important thing is for us to become very valuable to the community. As soon as our presence is desirable, the circumstances in which scholarly work can be carried out will be easy to establish . . . The University cannot be a construction company or social service agency, but some elements are matched to the problems of society.[3]

Some of the latter elements and the ways that they might be packaged have been the subject of the last chapters. It should be emphasized that the capacity to contribute to community development and poverty problems is to be found in institutions wherever situated. Even though for colleges set in a sea of poverty, community improvement may sometimes seem a question of survival, the means and responsibilities for promoting development are not confined to inner-city institutions.

If the campus activities just described seem truly slender threads from which to weave a strong fabric of cooperation, they are to be viewed as preliminary to the major task. The whole cloth of communication and cooperation will be woven through mutually beneficial, autonomous, service projects.

The Process of Cooperation

Ways of proceeding with service programs in urban poverty areas have been traced in these last chapters. In essence, an ad hoc process of cooperation has been outlined instead of an a priori set of answers to the problems of the poor. Two distinctive organizational features have been emphasized throughout the discussion: (1) that the project be autonomous of the college, consumer-oriented, and whenever feasible, consumer-controlled; (2) that teaching and learning be integrated with the services extended by the college. When so structured, new programs of service avoid many of the pitfalls of existing programs and offer at least four kinds of concurrent benefits.

First, from the standpoint of community groups, the college or university offers the tools required for self-help and self-development. Thus, the services of a college would take varied forms according to local needs, ranging from helping the group to articulate its general goals in terms of specific objectives that can be implemented, to advising on appropriate ways to command funds from public or private sources, to offering indigenous leaders new learning experiences in development planning, organization and management. A decentralized, diversified, and, in a broad sense, a competitive set of locally responsive programs would emerge. The most successful elements derived from these multifold experiences provide guides to further improvements and could be replicated in other places.

Second, from a standpoint of a college, it gains a new arena for learning, with pedagogical situations well suited to some of its students. Old "Joe College" has passed away, with about 70% of contemporary college students attending public institutions, 83% in their home state, with only 30% living on campus in collegiate housing, and with two out of three as the first generation to go to college. For students seeking socially purposeful roles, new educational fare is offered in urban poverty areas.

Third, in professional fields, where existing criteria of technical competence are determined exclusively by peers in the profession, a second dimension inherent in public accountability is highlighted, that of social accountability. A second and larger framework for evaluating professional performance is introduced. In addition, autonomous, client-centered projects offer fresh opportunities for linkages between graduate departments and professional schools of the university and between universities and community colleges. New ways of focusing interdisciplinary research and eliciting interdisciplinary insights are provided.

Finally, collaborative projects that are autonomous of the college or university, besides encouraging self-determination by community groups, preserve institutional flexibility and independence. The commitment of an institution of higher learning to community ventures must be sustained, if it is to be effective, but it must also be terminable. It must be sustained long enough to determine and ensure the viability of the venture and terminable thereafter, when the project either takes root in the community, flourishing on its own, with independent sources of support, or is abandoned. Otherwise, community service projects in poverty areas can easily become bottomless pits, as recently established, neighborhood health centers have already demonstrated. Consumer-controlled community projects, however, avoid situations of structured dependency and also permit the institution to change its course with the passage of time and retreat from its level of commitment without hurting its neighbors.

11

Generating a Statewide and Metropolitan Response

Many policy questions related to the urban poor fall within the province of a single institution of higher learning or its faculty, but others involve statewide and systemwide policies. Issues in which statewide educational policies may be determinative are discussed in this chapter.

Cost Constraints

First and foremost for tax-supported colleges and universities are questions of cost and the allocation of resources. With the onset of economic recession coupled with inflation and budgetary cutbacks, fiscal problems have become a dominant concern. The bread-and-butter necessity of making ends meet is a key issue at the outset of the seventies. Ironically, the consequent necessity to re-evaluate priorities within and among institutions may prove a more potent factor in precipitating long overdue, specific reforms than any of the hot rhetoric of recent years.

While the exigencies of economy and efficiency have created the climate for self evaluation, questions of equity cannot be tabled. Unfortunately, there are no cheap ways to resolve poverty problems on their present scale, and there are no cheap ways for institutions of higher education to participate effectively in that task. If community service activities were to divert scarce resources from teaching and scholarship so as to dilute their quality, they would be self-defeating since mediocre institutions tend to produce mediocre, ineffectual programs.

Some of the proposals advanced in earlier chapters can be implemented at little additional cost; others entail significant increases in expenditures. When they are directed toward organizational and administrative procedures (as, for example, the rooting out of the vestiges of discrimination in employment and procurement or the calibration of junior and senior college curricula) added costs are minimal. In some cases, also, federal assistance may be available to finance experimental community programs, as in recreation, day care, or neighborhood service centers. In other cases, collaborative efforts with agencies already funded by state and local governments provide the staging area for innovations, as for example, in manpower training programs in several public service occupations. In contrast, to ensure that no qualified student is denied the opportunity for higher education for lack of money, increases in expenditure far beyond their present levels are required in state and federal scholarship, loan, and work-study financial aids, especially in the light of recent tuition raises and rising institutional costs.

The need for increased expenditures, particularly for undergraduate education, can be anticipated over the course of the decade. Both the college-age and college-going sector of the population will continue to grow until 1980. Add to these growth factors the additional pressures of inflated costs and the necessity to improve the quality of teaching and scholarship. Altogether, despite current trends in precisely the opposite direction, it is evident that expenditures for higher education should rise at a steady rate in the next few years just to maintain the present relative scale and quality of operations, to say nothing about reaching into the communities of the poor.

To expect, therefore, that higher education could make significant inroads on poverty without major allocations of state and federal funds for that express purpose appears unreasonable. Urban poverty and human development programs cannot be undertaken by institutions of higher education on anything but a tiny demonstration scale without substantially increased levels of state aid, except at the risk of debasing the performance of essential traditional functions. If public higher education is charged with the task of educating increasingly large numbers of disadvantaged youths and underemployed adults and of mounting innovative, model service programs in poverty areas, let it be clearly understood that it is undertaking a vital and additional social task. If it is asked, in essence, to attempt to repair the failures of other educational and social institutions, the level of state financial support should reflect the nature of the task. Special collegiate programs for the poor should receive one hundred per cent public funding until such time as the need for them is eliminated at its sources, through raising the performance of public school systems and state agencies.

Granted that the approaches to service in poverty areas advocated in this study promise to be least diversionary of scarce resources for higher education. Granted that the probabilities are greatly improved that programs for the poor will enhance learning and scholarship if they are integral to ongoing educational and scholarly pursuits and if they respond to the priorities and values of their sponsoring clients. Even so, added special programs necessarily expend faculty energies and institutional resources. Furthermore, among existing programs, a relatively small proportion of those classified as community service meet the above criteria, and only a relatively few are directed to the urban poor.

Consequently, policy questions are twofold, short term and long range. In the short run, when a large infusion of new money for special programs seems improbable, the questions are, first, how to mobilize resources within the present system more effectively and, second, how to achieve a balance more reflective of contemporary urban needs. In this context, the reappraisal and gradual phasing out of old programs and the redirection of resources committed, for example, to outdated forms of vocational education, agricultural and other established special-interest extension programs would release some funds for new urban programs in urban settings.

Such questions, however, carry one to the vital center of decision-making about priorities within institutions and across systems, questions far beyond the limits of this study but nonetheless fundamental to building responsive programs of service. The diversity, autonomy and decentralization that characterize higher education in the United States are sources of its vitality and strength and are crucial to fresh, flexible approaches. Yet, these strengths may have their counterpart in negative characteristics. They sometimes give rise to hermetic institutions, self-perpetuating, departmental rigidities, diffusion of leadership, and lack of public accountability, altogether formidable barriers to innovation and adaptations to contemporary conditions.

Even within the limiting fiscal perimeters of the here and now and perhaps spurred by motives of economy, many needed structural changes, both within institutions and across systems, can be undertaken to lay the groundwork for effective future programs. The report of the President's Task Force of Higher Education, released in 1970, addressed some of these issues. Although the Task Force did not focus on service for the poor as such, their brief and knowledgeable statement on the question of institutional priorities is of direct relevance to any effort to mobilize latent talents and skills in higher education.[1]

In some states, planning and coordinating boards for higher education can play a strategic role as catalysts to change and to building a systemic response to urban needs and the urban poor. Issues, priorities and political climates, however, vary greatly in different states. In some, policies fostering greater institutional autonomy would release fresh initiatives, while in others, stricter accountability for performance would promote socially responsive endeavors.

In every state, however, the surest and easiest way to evoke fresh initiatives is to offer financial assistance. What is nearly universal, however, is the meager flow of funds into urban programs relative to allocations for rural and technical programs. Consequently, the resources from such federal programs as Title I of the Higher Education Act of 1964, or from other current or contemplated federal, state or private foundation sources should be carefully husbanded and used only to seed a limited number of promising, new programs. Because support has been spread thin among numerous small-scale projects, demonstrable results have been exceptional. By sharply focusing on realistic goals and engaging selected faculty across institutions, more effective future programs can be devised in the pattern of the Model Cities concept.

For long-range planning, neither the structure of a system nor the level of federal or state funds committed to education can be viewed as fixed. Despite current fiscal constraints, a time-phased, gradually expanding commitment to reduce and then to eliminate inequality over the course of a generation is a feasible and essential goal of state educational policy. The long-range perspectives of planning for higher education provide a framework for a time-phased strategy and a system of priorities for attaining full equality of educational opportunity, beginning in the next academic year and moving forward deliberately with planned annual increments. Since administrative adaptations and considerable additional money are needed to mount effective programs for the poor, the organization of a state system and its financial base are both viewed as variables in the discussion that follows.

Statewide Priorities and Community Colleges

For the poor, any summary of short-term educational priorities would include, at least, the following items.

—financial aids for higher education, with special opportunity grants to qualified students;
—remedial education for youths and adults to eliminate functional illiteracy;
—cooperative work-study programs, open at any age, emphasizing allied health-care occupations, preservice and inservice training in human and public service occupations, and other revamped forms of vocational and technical education.

A number of community colleges are already extensively engaged in remedial and career education, but their curricula and quality of teaching vary greatly. Some career programs are designed quite narrowly, offering training for a specific job, not for an open-ended career in a broad occupational field; nor are they viewed as a way to reach and cultivate broadly the intellects and sensibilities of students who have been unresponsive to conventional modes of teaching. A few colleges have been outstanding pacesetters in new forms of vocational education, mounting model programs that might well be emulated by lower schools.

Since the community colleges are most accessible to the urban poor, financially, geographically, and academically, they are a frequent point of entry into higher education and a chief avenue for economic advancement. Consequently, education for employment should be emphasized. First, because its concrete focus suits the learning styles and desire for demonstrable achievement of many students. Second, job opportunities are, and will continue to be most plentiful at middle-range levels of responsibility and technical levels of skill. Third, about 70-85% of the students entering community colleges do not complete the baccalaureate degree anywhere. Finally, cooperative work-study career programs, in particular, suit the financial predicament and family situation of many potential students and can be most economical for educational institutions as well.

Yet, if the education offered for employment is conceived merely as job training, and not as education, it carries with it grave dangers of premature cloture of a student's development and future economic mobility. If functional education is not to become another cul-de-sac for the aspiring student who is poor or black, career programs must be reappraised and redesigned. The rethinking and revamping of education for employment is the first of several difficult roles that have been assigned to community colleges, and it raises the first of a series of questions as to the colleges' probable performance in the coming decade.

The community college can be for the poor of this generation what the comprehensive high school was earlier in the century, provided that elementary and secondary education are also improved over the course of the seventies and provided that it resists the temptation to imitate traditional liberal arts colleges. The community colleges, with the advantage of hindsight, presumably could also avoid the grave problems often found in comprehensive high schools, with rigidly stratified, internal educational tracks and with de facto segregation prevailing across school districts.

How many colleges will take a stance and carve for themselves an educational mission uniquely responsive to contemporary societal and local needs is problematic. The toughest educational tasks in innovative teaching and community service have been thrust upon them, tasks of great social consequence, for which their faculties and administrators may be quite unprepared. Indeed, some are even reluctant to discharge these tasks, harboring instead ambitions and images of prestigious senior colleges. Following the latter course inevitably leads to community colleges that are, in the language of W.B. Yeats, "pale images that yet, pale images beget."

Although teaching is the prime and unambiguous mission of a community college, contradictory trends are discernible even here. Apart from a new emphasis on race consciousness in all-black or all-chicano colleges and with a few outstanding exceptions, new approaches to teaching are as yet uncharacteristic of community colleges as a group. In fact, educational innovations have mostly originated in selective liberal arts colleges. On the one hand, community colleges enroll a growing number of students whose academic interests are uncertain and who are open to new kinds of learning experiences. On the other hand, they have been recruiting a growing number of faculty with doctorates, whose educational and life experiences have been largely limited to conventional graduate schools. Furthermore, with the anticipated upward surge in the supply of new Ph.D. graduates relative to job vacancies in senior colleges, pressures will diminish to leaven faculties with practitioners from outside of the academy or with nonaccredited, dedicated teachers of diverse backgrounds.

Similar discordancies are perceptible in the relations of many community colleges with local nonestablishment and powerless community groups. Since the community colleges are locally controlled and locally financed with matching state contributions and since many are very new, the degree of their involvement in educational programs for the poor is exceedingly uneven. Many have neither the leadership, know-how, nor commitment to reach out and meet the needs of the poor in their district even when the latter are few in number. Nor are the poor evenly distributed among the junior college districts.

The resolution of these countertrends is largely dependent, at this point, upon the leadership and resources of each individual college. Statewide policies are essential if fiscal and social inequalities are to be reduced and if the development of a stratified system, segregated by class and race, is to be prevented. The districts in which problems are concentrated are usually the very districts where resources to address them are often least adequate or have already been spoken for.

If the community colleges are to be statewide agents of educational opportunity and community service, policy determination cannot be left entirely to local boards whose decisions may have the effect of excluding or ignoring the poor. Correspondingly, if local colleges are to carry the burdens of fulfilling key statewide and national objectives as well as local ones, the share of the state in financing the community colleges must also be significantly enlarged. Three proposals are advanced for consideration.

—Statewide guidelines in policy areas crucial to equality of educational opportunity should be formulated and promulgated for local boards of community colleges, and technical information services about existing and future grants-in-aid for special programs should be centralized and made available to local colleges.
—The share of annual operating costs borne by the state relative to local contributions should be increased progressively over the course of the decade so that by 1980 the state's proportionate share is predominant.
—The full cost of educating students residing in poverty areas and attending community colleges should be assumed immediately by the state.

The deficiencies of urban elementary and high schools place a major social responsibility and a costly financial burden on urban community colleges in the coming years. As we have seen, many youths in the poor and black neighborhoods of the inner city, including high school graduates, have literacy problems serious enough to preclude their effective participation in the mainstream of society. As many as a quarter to a half of all youths in some urban poverty areas have neither employable skills nor can they acquire them easily without first learning how to read.

It would be far cheaper, relative to the high costs of remediation and manpower training programs and the heavy psychological costs of repeated failure, if every child learned the three Rs and acquired an employable skill at an early age and stage in his development (before age sixteen and the termination of compulsory school attendance). The flow of candidates for remedial education should be checked at its sources; preventive programs are needed as well as corrective ones. The same expertise and careful planning that generally goes into the preparation of master plans for higher education should be spent on the preparation of statewide master plans for urban elementary and high schools.

From the standpoint of state educational policies, master planning to improve urban schools should receive a very high priority. It should be undertaken immediately so that remedial and special education programs for the disadvantaged in public colleges can be phased out towards the end of the decade. A major investment now in renovating urban schools would be self-liquidating over the course of a generation. Otherwise, greatly increased expenditures in community colleges will be needed to provide a second chance to learn long into the foreseeable future.

Social Policy Research

A number of exemplary research projects built in conjunction with state and local governmental agencies can be found at state universities throughout the nation—a number sufficient to demonstrate their feasibility and value both to the institutions and the state. As these programs are presently organized, however, there is little assurance (1) that problems of high priority will be addressed; (2) that a commitment to these projects will be sustained over a long enough period to bring forth results; or (3) that these projects will be financed on a scale adequate to attract the best faculty talents to problem-solving endeavors.

The Social Science Research Council, in a survey of research in the behavioral and social sciences at major universities, found that at least two-thirds of the approximately 200 existing research and service institutes "are not primarily concerned with applied social research development, but, rather, they work to extend and continue the traditional academic work of the disciplinary departments or they draw upon the resources of two or more disciplines in the pursuit of primary academic objectives."[2] Altogether, they found that only 10% of behavioral and social scientists in major universities are associated with existing research institutes. With good reason, such institutes are largely dependent for their support upon the vagaries of short-term grants and contracts and can rarely control tenured faculty positions or the education of graduate students. Because of their marginal status within the university and their dependence on outside sources of support, mortality rates are very high.

On the other hand, several of these institutes have stepped into a breach, and they are addressing major problems that the disciplines and professional schools tend to bypass. "The institutes' successes, in some cases, lie in their very willingness to attack problems that others have neglected in their research: urban problems, poverty, delinquency, conservation of resources, and the impact of technology on society."[3] A significant core of faculty can be found in every institution who would gladly participate in research on critical policy questions—faculty anxious to test and attune their methodology to actual social behavior.

A vehicle to link latent faculty resources at state colleges and universities with state problems is needed in many regions. Institutes of Government, existing now at state universities such as in North Carolina, Georgia or Illinois, often have close liaisons with state agencies or legislatures. However, they are largely staffed by political scientists and lawyers and tend to concentrate on administration, laws, justice, public finance and revenue issues, usually offering training programs to government officials in public administration. Valuable as these public services may be, a void in many vital social policy fields remains unfilled, and a more comprehensive mechanism, embracing other social and behavioral sciences and other professions would seem appropriate. An Institute for Social Policy Research could be created with state funds to provide a focus for multidisciplinary, interinstitutional research on major social problems in urban areas.

The establishment of a social policy institute at the state level offers a way to combine, with advantage, tendencies observable both in state government and in higher education. At universities, the growing interest in social policy questions leads inevitably to the convergence of teaching, research and public service. In fact, a recent study of graduate education in the social sciences, conducted at Columbia University by Paul F. Lazarsfeld and Samuel D. Sieber, recommended that responsibility for graduate education be transferred entirely to interdisciplinary research institutes after a first year of introductory studies in traditional academic departments.[4] They call for the creation of a series of research institutes as integral parts of the university, each institute concentrating on a particular social problem area, such as education, urban affairs, international relations, crime and delinquency, mass communication, and the environment. The Social Science Research Council, in the study cited earlier, also goes on to recommend the creation of a graduate school of applied behavioral sciences.

The committee recommends that universities consider the establishment of broadly based training and research programs in the form of a Graduate School of Applied Behavioral Science (or some local equivalent) under the administration arrangements that lie outside the established disciplines. Such training and research should be multidisciplinary (going beyond the behavioral and social sciences as necessary), and the school should accept responsibility for contributing through its research both to a basic understanding of human relationships and behavior and to the solution of persistent social problems.[5]

Apart from organizational details or the enormous difficulties inherent in totally restructuring graduate education, the thrust of both recommendations reflect similar, widely held dissatisfactions, and both are consonant with the more modest proposal advanced here. An Institute for Social Policy Research can be created promptly and relatively easily; if successful, it can eventually lead to the evolution of full-blown, multidisciplinary, policy-oriented graduate schools.

A different set of impulses, perceptible within state government, gives rise to and highlights the need for an independent agency for long-range social policy research. With rapidly rising state expenditures in human service fields and the growing complexity of state programs, efforts are underway in several leading states to systematize budgetary procedures, to develop rational criteria for the allocation of state resources and objective evaluation procedures with policy-oriented information systems, in short, a long-range state planning capability. Research and demonstration programs on specific problems have been funded by state governments, as well as those conducted under the aegis of federal agencies.[a]

An institute of wide scope and mission is needed in higher education to call forth multidisciplinary, interinstitutional work on a host of state problems. An institute, autonomous of state government, would be somewhat more insulated from immediate political pressures than state planning agencies. It could undertake research with longer time horizons and careful, experimental designs, with planned controls and predetermined evaluative criteria.

The particular scope, mission and location of such an institute would differ among the states, dependent upon local circumstances and problems, but a few, relatively universal, desirable features can be delineated. The institute should be independent of existing colleges and universities, being directly responsible to the executive arm of state government or the coordinating board for higher education, and drawing on faculty strengths scattered throughout the state system in a variety of professions and disciplines. The institute should have headquarters on or near the campus of the leading state university to take advantage of existing facilities, faculty resources, and libraries. When that university is not located in the state's chief city, at the center of its social problems and intellectual life, as in Michigan or Illinois, the locational choice is more difficult. In the latter state, the Circle Campus of the University of Illinois in Chicago, for example, might be a logical site. The institute's staff should be small since it will not con-

---

[a]One of the most interesting of these experimental projects is to be found in Illinois and, coincidentally, bears the name "Institute for Social Policy," although its purposes and structure differ somewhat from the institute proposed in this study for higher education. Although its mandate is exceptionally broad, the operations of the Illinois Institute for Social Policy illustrates trends found in many states. It was funded in Spring 1969, with an annual appropriation of $3.3 million from the state legislature "to develop, demonstrate and evaluate ways to improve services relating to manpower, health, public assistance and related services. . ." Under its auspices, a number of studies have been generated relating to health maintenance, management and administration, public service jobs, and slum housing, but the Institute has also set up three demonstration programs. The first, in Woodlawn, a poverty area just south of the University of Chicago, is testing new methods for rendering public assistance and state services, through the separation of income maintenance from service programs, and through community involvement in planning and the coordination of state services under one roof. The second project, located in Peoria, with comparable aims and features, is directed toward testing these in a low density, tricounty, downstate area. The third and newest project is a joint one between a community college, Malcolm X, and a state juvenile correctional institution, St. Charles Training School for Boys. Its purpose is to determine the effects of improved educational opportunities on recidivism.

duct research itself but is conceived as a means of enlisting faculty and students into innovative research and demonstration projects on widespread state problems. One thinks, for example, of public education, welfare or urban redevelopment, of problems in these fields that tend to be the exclusive province of professional educators, social workers or urban planners, but which need an infusion of new insights from other disciplines if they are to be resolved. A series of parallel, controlled, demonstration projects in different locations to test new approaches can be envisioned.

The institute can serve several simultaneous purposes. First, it is a vehicle through which state research funds on urban problems can be channeled more rationally and allocated more carefully. Second, it can assist state coordinating boards for higher education and state colleges in their deliberations about priorities in community service. Third, with the growing complexity of state programs, it can provide an ongoing, objective evaluative capability for appraising new experiences. Fourth, it could seed and conduct demonstration projects in poverty areas, where responsible community groups are as yet absent (projects that might be imprudent for a single institution to undertake alone). Finally, it offers a means to underwrite and encourage faculty and graduate student research in dispersed locations.

As for the latter, it should be recognized that although the centralization of basic research and related academic degree programs is essential to ensure quality, many forms of action-oriented research and training can be decentralized with advantage. The faculties of small colleges and new universities should be able to participate in large-scale, joint, problem-solving endeavors with colleagues in their own fields of specialization or other related disciplines. Research support for faculty in developing universities is needed to facilitate the recruitment of able people and for its indirect effects, both on the quality and relevance of their teaching and the quality of regional, community service programs.

Although there is no assurance that social research organized in this manner would be productive, the prospects are good. A recent retrospective study of major advances in the social and behavioral sciences since 1900 found "indisputable evidence of the cumulative growth of knowledge," and, even though the study was not keyed to the applications of research, it also found that three-fourths of the advances were stimulated by practical social demands.[6] Most major new developments during the last four decades have emerged from teams of scholars working in a relatively few intellectual centers where, in the authors' opinions, there is "a certain critical mass in terms of intellectual powers and resources, ready access to mathematics, computers, laboratories, specialists in other fields, and complex urban cultures." They recommended that future research be supported at a limited number of major centers. They further recommended that it be staged in ten- to fifteen-year programs in order to consolidate advances, since they found that the first impact of new knowledge has been generally delayed by about ten to fifteen years.

Metropolitan Perspectives

A study relating to urban poverty inevitably focuses on the largest cities, the growing regional capitals across the nation. These centers of economic power and intellectual life are also the seat of sharply contrasting, densely concentrated poverty areas. It is in the largest cities, as well, that the accomplishments and deficiencies of state systems of higher education are thrown into sharp relief.

The extraordinary expansion of public higher education in the last decade has brought unprecedented opportunities for education, opportunities readily seized by many working-class and minority group students. The arrival on campus of students variously described with such attractive adjectives as disadvantaged, ethnic, lowest quartile or nonelite, is a powerful force for change, as yet only partially appreciated and absorbed. The bright accomplishments of state systems have a dark side which is most evident in the largest metropolitan areas.

Paradoxically, as the gates of higher education have been unlocked, the inequalities prevailing in the larger society have been carried into the very systems most open to receive them. One finds, in consequence, institutions in three-tiered, state systems of high education, presently developing into reasonably accurate facsimiles of the three top tiers of a multitiered society. One finds the racially and socially segregated patterns of urban settlement settling into the commuter colleges as students are sorted out geographically. One finds the anomolous fiscal and economic disparities within metropolitan areas, reflecting antiquated township and county lines, and the urban-suburban-rural imbalances, reflecting the composition of state legislatures, similarly reflected in the allocation of resources for public institutions of higher education. Were present trends to continue, the same inequalities and educational problems associated with racial and social segregation now found in urban high schools would rapidly descend with their students upon urban public colleges.

Social trends, of course, are not destiny. State systems of higher education can alter the not so inexorable course of events and in their policies, deliberately attempt to rewrite the scenario. In Philadelphia, New York, Detroit, Los Angeles, Chicago and every other major city where the poor and the blacks mostly live in identifiable neighborhoods of the central city, metropolitanwide policies are lacking in virtually every public issue, whether housing, schools, taxation, recreation or health.

In contrast, higher educational policies can be built upon rational, empirical criteria that take account of inherent, metropolitan linkages and effects. Because of historical, socioeconomic, political and geographic variations among the great cities, the impairments and imbalances in higher educational systems are quite different, but the need for a metropolitan frame of reference in developing equitable programs for the urban poor is universal. To illustrate urban imbalances that typically emerge and concrete policies that would emanate from a metropolitan stance, the public system in Chicago is used as a case study.

Higher Education in Metropolitan Chicago

When one thinks comprehensively about the Illinois public system of higher education, what it achieves or fails to achieve and how it might be improved, Chicago is a chief point of reference. Two-thirds of the college-age population in Illinois lives in the Chicago area, while colleges located in Chicago account for only one-half of the total enrollments in all public colleges.

In issues related to urban poverty, the Chicago region is of special concern since most of the poor and minority groups of the state live in its largest city. More than 1.3 million blacks, about 86.3% of those in Illinois, reside in the Chicago area, and two-thirds of all recipients of public assistance, including three-fourths of those receiving aid to families with dependent children, are also concentrated in Chicago. Almost half the population of the central city is nonwhite or Spanish-speaking. As we have seen in Chapter 2, these demographic patterns are characteristic of large metropolitan areas, and so are many of the problems in public higher education.

Dysfunctional features or gaps in public higher education in metropolitan Chicago are to be observed mostly (1) at its base in the community colleges; (2) at its pinnacle where noticeable gaps in graduate and professional education remain; and (3) across institutions in the lack of connective tissue. As we have seen, each of these elements is exceedingly important to the quality of educational and service programs in poverty areas, and each will be discussed in turn.

The community colleges in metropolitan Chicago are the chief vehicles for extending educational opportunities to disadvantaged youths and impoverished adults, enrolling, for example, two out of five of all lower-division black students attending state colleges.[7] The extent of involvement of different colleges in the region, however, varies widely, and only a tiny proportion of nonwhite students go to suburban colleges (Tables 6-1, 6-2, and 6-4). The recommendations offered earlier regarding increased state participation in setting policy guidelines and financing locally controlled, community colleges so as to assure open-door, effective programs for the poor, are especially applicable to metropolitan Chicago.

The present organization of community colleges in metropolitan Chicago tends to produce uneconomical, inequitable and discriminatory effects. The City Colleges of Chicago provide educational opportunities for most of the disadvantaged and minority students in the region and state, but their position is anomalous. The colleges in the city system have neither close ties with a single, local community area nor comprehensive regional authority with funds adequate to finance the education of large numbers of disadvantaged, inner-city students. In the suburban ring, each local college board makes separate decisions that altogether materially affect the climate of opportunity in the region as a whole.

A pattern of community colleges differentiated by class and race, has emerged in the region. The presumed advantages of the neighborhood school seem very slight for young and mature adults when balanced against their discriminatory, insulating effects. The organization of the community college network in metropolitan Chicago should be reviewed and revised with a view toward providing access ultimately for any student to any community college in the region and toward providing a more widely based, equitable system of funding and governance.

As for graduate and professional education, the public universities in metropolitan Chicago do not as yet offer a comprehensive educational array at graduate and professional levels so that opportunities for low-cost, advanced studies by mature, able, commuter students are relatively limited. In addition, without a strong, resident graduate faculty, the quality and scope of possible multidisciplinary, problem-oriented research and demonstration projects for the poor are also necessarily constrained. While several, distinguished, private universities are located in metropolitan Chicago, and, considered together, do offer a range of doctoral and professional degree programs, their students are frequently drawn from across the nation, indeed, the world. Nor can it be assumed that their faculties will concern themselves with state and local problems.

Senior colleges recently established or enlarged in metropolitan Chicago have redressed, somewhat, the historical rural imbalance in the public system and are beginning to meet acute local needs for higher education at the undergraduate level. The state system, viewed regionally however, resembles a mountain without a summit, or perhaps a very irregular one. One thinks in this connection of the graduate schools at Circle Campus, which is the hub of the regional system geographically and its capstone strategically and, only to a lesser degree, of the smaller developing universities. Paradoxically, while Circle Campus has been evolving into the full-blown public university that has been lacking in Chicago, several of the departments at Circle Campus most relevant to urban social policy questions have been slow to develop graduate faculties with related expertise. This may prove to be fortuitous since the opportunity still exists in a few fields, and should be seized, to recruit a special kind of faculty that will share a commitment to the goals of an urban public university and whose scholarly interests coincide with them. For example, an economist concerned with the application of quantitative techniques to the evaluation of policies and programs is more likely to become involved in urban social policy research than one who is mostly interested in corporate conglomerates.

In enlarging the opportunities for graduate education in the Chicago region, an early priority should be given to the social and behavioral sciences since, to profit from the emerging experience, research and evaluative components should be built into every innovative service program. The recent softening of academic job markets calls into question prevailing projections indicating a need to train more social scientists to man faculty posts as college enrollments expand and to conduct future social research and action programs.[b] Even without a major expansion in graduate education in the social sciences, a greater proportion of existing resources should be relocated in Chicago, where a strong social science capability is essential to devise and appraise service programs and to staff a variety of other critical, consultative, and educational positions. Doctoral and professional degree programs in the Chicago region should be progressively expanded so that, by 1980, a comprehensive array of advanced studies in the liberal arts and the professions will be available to commuter students, with early priorities given to the social and behavioral sciences and the health sciences.

As for interinstitutional, coordinate policies or joint endeavors, there are few among the public colleges in Chicago. Impediments to effective responses to the needs of the poor that are repeatedly observed in the system, arise largely from the fact that, viewed regionally, there is, in effect, no formal system at all. Without a comprehensive, regional framework for joint policy planning, neighboring institutions at different levels in the hierarchy of higher education must improvise coordinative mechanisms, issue by issue, field by field. One could continue to address issues in this piecemeal fashion. Alternatively, it is possible, in one stroke, to create a new regional layer of administration to deal comprehensively with the cluster of problems in the coming years.

Some sort of coordinative mechanism seems essential in the Chicago region if only because of its size and density. Over 7 1/2 million people live in close proximity, two-thirds of the state's population. With well-developed transportation networks, many persons have physical, if not actual, access to a number of the public institutions of higher learning and perceive their options in terms of a system. Reorganization at the community college level was suggested earlier as desirable in any case, without reference to the question of the relationship of the junior to senior institutions.

Conceivably, a new informal or formal, horizontal, coordinative body for all Chicago institutions could be placed athwart the present state governance systems, most of which are organized along hierarchical-historical lines rather than regional ones, except for Southern Illinois University. Inserting an additional policy-making body into the existing framework, however, might compound the difficulties of joint planning.

Thinking of the long-term course of development of higher education, the opportunity exists now to reconstruct the system; public higher education on a large scale is still evolving in Chicago and is relatively new, compared, let us say, with the system in New York City. It is therefore appropriate to question wheth-

[b]The Illinois Board of Higher Education, Committee R on Graduate Education in the Social Sciences, in 1969, found that "As of the mid-Sixties, the non-public universities of the state were the source of about three-fifths of all M.A. degrees and three-fourths of all Ph.D. degrees awarded in the social sciences in the state." The Committee suggested that by 1980, graduate enrollments in public universities should be increased threefold at the master's degree over those in 1965 and quadrupled at the doctoral level.

er the present structures of governance work well or whether reassemb/
component institutions into a totally new system of metropolitan gov/
might be preferable.

What principles might determine the form of a new regional system'
pattern of administration for higher education could take cognizance oi seveiai
important aspects of contemporary cities that few governmental or functional
agencies operating in metropolitan areas anywhere in the nation have as yet con-
fronted successfully.

First, there is the difficult question of centralization and decentralization of
decision-making in every field. Which functions are best reserved for community
area decision-making in order to ensure widespread participation in building
responsive policies. Which programs and functions are invested with such wide
social significance and regional consequences that decision-making must be centralized? In higher education, among the latter kinds of policy issues, one thinks,
for example, of questions about tuitions and financial aids, admissions criteria,
standards of excellence or even locational decisions and, among the former,
emphasis in curricula or service programs in community colleges.

Second, a rational system of metropolitan governance could take into account the functional unity of labor markets and communications networks and
the economic interdependence of community areas in the metropolitan region.
It would intentionally disregard artificial boundaries between city, suburb, and
hinterland when not germane to the issues. Half the population of metropolitan
Chicago lives in its suburban ring, half in the central city, and the urban fringe is
rapidly being developed.

Third, a forward-looking system could take into account the enormous socioeconomic and fiscal disparities among residential community areas, arising largely from segregation in housing and zoning practices. It could deliberately com-
pensate for the resultant inequalities in opportunity.

How might a new system be organized in the Chicago area? One could en-
vision, for example, a regional system of public higher education whose perimeters would be determined by actual urban settlement and commuting patterns.
Within this region, which would be large and very populous, three subregional
units for administration might be created, to the south, the north, and the west.
The Circle Campus and Medical School of the University of Illinois and the Loop
College of the City Colleges of Chicago, because of their central locations or
functions, should be excluded from the subregional divisions, although no other
university is as yet situated in the western sector of Chicago.

These wedged-shaped, subregional sectors would stretch from the outer rim
of the Loop to the urban fringe, crossing city and town lines and following
major transportation arteries. Boundaries for each would be drawn expressly to
include a variety of community areas, inhabited by black and white, poor, working-class and rich persons. Each level of higher education would be available in
each sector, at least one public senior institution and a number of community

colleges, with the exception of doctoral and advanced professional degree programs which would be concentrated in the central area.

Within each subregion, liaisons and responsibilities of senior to junior institutions for faculty and curricula development could be carefully defined and dovetailed by each university in consultation with its related community colleges. Access to courses in any of the community colleges would be open to all students, and upon successful completion of a requisite course of study, admission to the senior college would be guaranteed.[c] Although formal, subregional organizational patterns and guidelines might be standardized, the autonomy and distinctive identity of each college and university within subregional constellations would be emphasized and preserved in order to provide genuine alternatives to students. Diverse ways of achieving shared educational and service objectives enrich the common pool of experience.

This pattern of organization would accomplish at least four simultaneous purposes. First, it would be economical since costly technical facilities and specialized faculties could be centralized and duplication minimized among the colleges. Second, it would foster a socially and racially integrated student mix. Third, it would enhance the quality of educational and service programs in poverty areas by ensuring close linkages between senior and junior institutions in the same territory. Fourth, the need for costly special educational programs for disadvantaged students at senior colleges might also be minimized if community college students were permitted joint registration and access to some of the courses in the senior institution in the sector (with guaranteed admission on the satisfactory completion of a prescribed number of basic courses). The student himself would set the pace, and counselling services would be available to all institutions. University students could avail themselves of technical or remedial courses at community colleges as well through joint registration. For example, a university student who was planning to teach a technical or vocational subject might take a course offered only at a community college. University faculty and students would also have a ready-made base in nearby community colleges for cooperative internship and research programs in poverty areas.

All these objectives can be achieved in a variety of other ways, several of which have been suggested elsewhere in this study. The above example of an alternative system of governance and administration has been put forward with purpose. It has been deliberately spelled out to widen the frame of reference in which the issues raised throughout this study relating to service in poverty areas are to be considered. The severity and concentration of poverty problems in urban areas are of such magnitude that only an institutionalized, long-term, systemwide commitment to address them is likely to bring positive results.

---

[c]To spur efficiency and widen opportunity, the State University of New York announced a major reorganization of the system in Fall, 1971, including the division of its 72 campuses into 8 administrative regions outside of New York City. Under the new system, the University would guarantee any community college graduate, outside of New York City, admission to a senior college in his region, starting in Fall, 1974. City University of New York also guarantees admission to senior colleges to its community college graduates.

Appendixes

Appendix A
Measuring Poverty

Two general ways of measuring the extent of poverty should be distinguished: one uses a fixed income level as its standard, the other a relative standard. Each method answers somewhat different questions in a policy context. The percentages of United States families classified as poor since World War II (calculated against fixed and relative standards of measurement) are presented in Table A-1.

It can be seen that the relative distribution of personal income shares

Table A-1
Percentage of United States Families Classified Poor by Changing and Fixed Standards, 1947 to 1965 (in 1965 dollars)

Year	Percentage of Families	
	Income Less Than One-half the Median	Income Less Than $3,000
1947	18.9%	30.0%
1948	19.1	31.2
1949	20.2	32.3
1950	20.0	29.9
1951	18.9	27.8
1952	18.9	26.3
1953	19.8	24.6
1954	20.9	26.2
1955	20.0	23.6
1956	19.6	21.5
1957	19.7	21.7
1958	19.8	21.8
1959	20.0	20.6
1960	20.3	20.3
1961	20.3	20.1
1962	19.8	18.9
1963	19.9	18.0
1964	19.9	17.1
1965	20.0	16.5

Source: Victor R. Fuchs, "Comment on Measuring the Low-Income Population," in *Six Papers on the Size Distribution of Wealth and Income*, edited by Lee Soltow (National Bureau of Economic Research, 1969), p. 200.

(Column 1) has not changed significantly in decades. Indeed, the overall pattern of income distribution in the United States after World War II has been one of the most stable of all social or economic statistics. No evidence of progress toward reducing differentials in the incomes of the lowest fifth compared with the national average can be found. While little alteration of the basic income class structure in the nation is observed, in contrast, overall levels of income and standards of living have risen considerably with continuing national economic growth (Column 2). Consequently, the numbers and percentages of families with annual incomes under $3,000 have steadily declined. If one is interested primarily in income maintenance policies, the concept of a fixed poverty line reflecting a minimum income for a tolerable standard of living has validity. But for educational institutions, also concerned with long-range progress toward reducing inequality in relative standards of living, patterns of income distribution are equally significant.

Most of the federal studies measuring the extent of poverty employ the concept of a fixed standard of real income, usually determined by ascertaining the cost of a minimum subsistence diet, adjusted to take account of different household sizes and rural-urban cost-of-living differentials. For an urban family of four in 1969, for example, the poverty level or line was designated by the Social Security Administration at an annual income near $3,700, compared with urban median family incomes estimated nationally at about $9,000 and with the $9,600 income level indicated by the Bureau of Labor Statistics as required for a moderate standard of living for a four-person household. Alternatively sometimes, an annual family income of below $3,000 is used as a rough indicator of poverty. It should be stressed that a poverty line, however determined, is a socially defined, abstract construct and a crude one which takes no account of such important factors as savings, home ownership, capital accumulation or intermittancy of employment.

Appendix B
Urbanization, Poverty and Race in Illinois

Known throughout the world for its bounteous agricultural exports and its fertile corn fields, Illinois is in reality a highly urbanized state, the most urbanized in the Midwest. Its population in 1970 totalled more than 11.1 million persons and four out of five of its citizens, 78.7%, lived in metropolitan counties (Table B-1). Three out of five, or 61.7% resided in the Chicago area. There are presently nine cities in Illinois large enough to be designated metropolitan areas (SMSA) by the Census Bureau. A host of other smaller cities dot the prairie and river banks of the state, but none of the metropolitan areas or cities, other than Chicago, contains more than 5% of the state's population. Of the rural population in Illinois, it is estimated that only 4% are actually engaged in farming, compared with about 5% for the nation as a whole, the balance residing in small cities and towns.[a]

The urbanization of this state has been largely funneled into its northeast corner, with almost four-fifths or 78.8% of the metropolitan population of the state living in a single metropolitan center. But even these statistics for the six-county SMSA of Chicago understate the degree of urbanization since Chicago is the center of a regional economy, with well-established industrial and communication linkages spilling over county and state boundaries into Indiana and Wisconsin.

Looking at the growth of the state as a whole during the sixties, urbanization continued in accordance with national trends, with metropolitan areas capturing most of the population increase. Between 1960 and 1970 the total population of the state increased by 10.2% at a slower rate than the 13.3% nationwide increase. The SMSAs grew most rapidly, increasing by 12.2%, while population in the balance of the state rose only slightly, about 2.9%. The suburbs of Chicago and Peoria and the cities of Rockford, Bloomington-Normal and Champaign-Urbana grew most rapidly, but the two latter cities are college towns whose population counts include resident students. Although the population increase in the Midwest was slower than in the West or Southwest, urban growth, particularly in the suburban ring, has shown no signs of decelerating.

The rise and fall of cities in the United States is closely related to their economic development. People tend to follow jobs. The shadow of lingering poverty falls all the more starkly against the powerful performance of the economy of the Chicago area. As the capital of steel and heavy metals with a diversified industrial base, Chicago's economic output is surpassed by only ten nations in the world. For example, Austria, with approximately the same population as Chi-

---

[a]According to the estimate of Illinois Cooperative Area Manpower Planning System, for Fiscal 1970, there were 434,370 farm workers in Illinois in 1968.

149

Table B-1
Population in Illinois by Standard Metropolitan Statistical Area (SMSA)[1] and County, 1960-1970

	Population–1970		Population–1960		Increase 1960–70	
	Number of Persons	Percent of Illinois Total	Number of Persons	Percent of Illinois Total	Number of Persons	Percent
Illinois	11,113,976	100.0%	10,081,158	100.0%	1,032,818	10.2%
Illinois SMSAs	8,903,065	80.1%	7,933,031	78.7%	970,034	12.2%
Bloomington-Normal[2]	104,389	.9%	83,877	.8%	20,512	24.5%
McLean	104,389	.9%	83,877	.8%	20,512	24.5%
Champaign-Urbana	163,281	1.5%	132,436	1.3%	30,845	23.3%
Champaign	163,281	1.5%	132,436	1.3%	30,845	23.3%
Chicago	6,978,947	62.8%	6,220,913	61.7%	758,034	12.2%
Cook	5,492,369	49.4%	5,129,725	50.9%	362,644	7.1%
DuPage	491,882	4.4%	313,459	3.1%	178,423	56.9%
Kane	251,005	2.3%	208,246	2.1%	42,759	20.5%
Lake	382,638	3.4%	293,656	2.9%	88,982	30.3%
McHenry	111,555	1.0%	84,210	.8%	27,345	32.5%
Will	249,498	2.2%	191,617	1.9%	57,881	30.2%
Decatur	125,010	1.1%	118,257	1.2%	6,753	5.7%
Macon	125,010	1.1%	118,257	1.2%	6,753	5.7%

East St. Louis	536,110	4.8%	487,198	4.8%	48,912	10.0%
Madison	250,934	2.3%	224,689	2.2%	26,245	11.7%
St. Clair	285,176	2.6%	262,509	2.6%	22,667	8.6%
Peoria	341,979	3.1%	313,412	3.1%	28,567	9.1%
Peoria	195,318	1.8%	189,044	1.9%	6,274	3.3%
Tazewell	118,649	1.1%	99,789	1.0%	18,860	18.9%
Woodford[3]	28,012	0.3%	24,579	.2%	3,433	14.0%
Rockford	272,063	2.4%	230,091	2.3%	41,972	18.2%
Boone[3]	25,440	.2%	20,326	.2%	5,114	25.2%
Winnebago	246,623	2.2%	209,765	2.1%	36,858	17.6%
Rock Island	219,951	2.0%	200,308	2.0%	19,643	9.8%
Rock Island	166,734	1.5%	150,991	1.5%	15,743	10.4%
Henry[3]	53,217	.5%	49,317	.5%	3,900	7.9%
Springfield	161,335	1.5%	146,539	1.5%	14,796	10.1%
Sangamon	161,335	1.5%	146,539	1.5%	14,796	10.1%
Illinois excluding SMSAs	2,210,911	19.9%	2,148,127	21.3%	62,784	2.9%

[1] An SMSA is a county or group of contiguous counties which contains at least one city of 50,000 inhabitants or more, or "twin cities" with a combined population of at least 50,000.

[2] Not SMSA in 1960.

[3] Not included in SMSA in 1960.

Source: U.S. Bureau of Census, 1970.

cago, had a gross national product of about $6 billion while the gross national product of the Chicago area was estimated in 1969 at approximately $44 billion.[1] Thus, statistically, Chicago has characteristically sustained lower average unemployment rates than either the state or nation as a whole, and higher median family incomes than most of the nation's largest cities.

As the center of an intricate state and interstate regional economic and communications network, Chicago is also the seat of major state and national social problems. Both the wealth and the urban problems of the state are heavily concentrated along the shores of Lake Michigan, so that the disparities in living conditions in neighboring community areas emerge in sharp relief.

In 1960, 13% of the families in Illinois had incomes below $3,000, as compared with 20.3% in the nation as a whole, and Illinois, a highly productive state, ranked third among the states in per capita personal income. Since then, although the 1970 income data by community areas are unavailable, the total number of poor families in Illinois has probably declined, as they have throughout the nation, and Illinois ranks fifth in per capita personal income.

Although families with low incomes are to be found throughout the state, particularly elderly white families, the preponderance of poor families live in urban areas and in a few rural counties. Of all Illinois families with annual incomes under $4,000 in 1960, more than two out of three, 69.4%, lived in metropolitan areas, and half lived in the Chicago area, 49.6%.[2] Since then, poverty has continued to migrate with the people to metropolitan areas.

Within the Chicago metropolitan area, families with low incomes are heavily concentrated in a few suburban towns and in a limited number of central-city community areas. The incidence of high unemployment follows a similar pattern (Table B-2). The contrast of median family income among rich and poor and black and white community areas in metropolitan Chicago is immediately apparent. Median family income for the entire Chicago SMSA in 1966, for example, was estimated at $9,400—at $8,100 in the city and $10,500 in the suburban ring. But the disparity was very great between median family incomes in the top ten white suburbs ($22,330) and in the ten poorest black areas within the city ($4,809).[3]

In metropolitan Chicago, income differentials by race tend to be narrower than in the nation, but in the mid-sixties, median incomes of black families were approximately one-third lower than those of whites. In 1966, for example, median incomes of white families in the Chicago SMSA were estimated at $9,900 and of black families at $6,100.[4] In East St. Louis, which was 70% black in 1968, the close association of poverty and race could also be observed. Of the families living in the Model Cities area, 51.6% had annual incomes under $3,000 and 82.2% under $7,000.[5]

If public aid statistics are used as a crude indicator of contemporary poverty in Illinois, the urban concentration of poor families is even more pronounced. In January 1970, of all recipients of public aid under the five established programs,

Table B-2

Unemployment in Illinois and Chicago, 1969

| | (Number in thousands) | | |
	Total Labor Force	Number of Unemployed	Unemployment Rate
Illinois			
Total	4,590	132	2.9
Men 20 years and over	2,620	43	1.6
Women 20 years and over	1,550	42	2.7
Both sexes, 16-19 years	420	47	11.2
White	4,120	102	2.5
Nonwhite	470	30	6.4
Chicago			
SMSA:			
Total	2,840	85	3.0
Men 20 years and over	1,610	26	1.6
Women 20 years and over	980	27	2.8
Both sexes, 16-19	250	32	13.0
White	2,470	61	2.5
Nonwhite	370	23	6.2
Central City:			
Total	1,370	47	3.4
White	1,040	27	2.6
Nonwhite	330	20	5.9

Source: U.S. Bureau of Labor Statistics.

84.7% lived in metropolitan areas, 69.1% in the Chicago area and 7.8% in the East St. Louis area (Table B-3). Of families with dependent children receiving public aid, a more significant figure perhaps in terms of educational policies, 89.8% lived in metropolitan areas, 74.5% of these in the Chicago area, primarily in Cook County, and 8.5% in the East St. Louis area (Table B-4).

In Illinois and in all major industrial states, public aid rolls have been soaring in recent years. It is not to be assumed that the rapid expansion in public assistance necessarily represents an increase in the actual number of poor persons but, instead, may reflect more extensive coverage by the program within the pool of poor families. Most of the new recipients in Illinois are women and children living in Cook County.

Table B-3

Public Aid in Illinois for Total of Five Programs by SMSA and County, January 1970[a]

SMSA and County	Number of Recipients	Recipients per 1,000 Population[b]	Recipients in Area as Percent of Total in Illinois
Illinois Total	592,493	54	100.0
Illinois SMSAs	501,594	57	84.7
Bloomington-Normal			
McLean	1,970	22	.3
Champaign-Urbana			
Champaign	3,961	26	.7
Chicago	409,250	59	69.1
Cook	393,148	71	66.4
DuPage	2,409	6	.4
Kane	3,718	15	.6
Lake	4,748	13	.8
McHenry	1,025	10	.2
Will	4,202	18	.7
Decatur			
Macon	7,331	58	1.2
East St. Louis	46,334	86	7.8
Madison	11,098	44	1.9
St. Clair	35,236	122	5.9
Peoria	12,169	35	2.1
Peoria	8,951	44	1.5
Tazewell	2,697	23	.5
Woodford	521	19	.1
Rockford	8,656	31	1.5
Boone	296	12	—
Winnebago	8,360	33	1.4
Rock Island	5,369	25	.9
Henry	892	17	.2
Rock Island	4,477	28	.8
Springfield			
Sangamon	6,554	41	1.1
Illinois excluding SMSAs	90,899	41	15.3

[a]The five programs included are: (1) General Assistance; (2) Old Age Assistance; (3) Aid to Dependent Children; (4) Blind Assistance; and (5) Disability.

[b]Population estimates used are from the Department of Public Health for July 1, 1968, and are based on total population by county.

Source: State of Illinois Department of Public Aid.

Table B-4

Aid to Families with Dependent Children in Illinois by SMSA and County, January 1970

SMSA and County	Number of Recipients	Children per 1,000 Population (1968)	Percent Recipients in Area of Total in Illinois
Illinois Total	390,525	35.5	100.0
Illinois SMSAs	350,598	39.9	89.8
Bloomington-Normal			
McLean	769	8.5	.2
Champaign-Urbana			
Champaign	2,622	17.5	.7
Chicago	290,880	42.3	74.5
Cook	282,131	51.2	72.2
DuPage	1,144	2.7	.3
Kane	1,633	6.5	.4
McHenry	611	6.0	.2
Will	2,670	11.3	.7
Decatur			
Macon	4,322	34.2	1.1
East St. Louis	33,301	61.8	8.5
Madison	6,613	26.3	1.7
St. Clair	26,688	92.7	6.8
Peoria	7,441	21.3	1.9
Peoria	5,709	27.8	1.5
Tazewell	1,566	13.4	.4
Woodford	166	6.2	–
Rockford	5,903	21.1	1.5
Boone	163	6.7	–
Winnebago	5,740	22.5	1.5
Rock Island	2,644	12.5	.7
Henry	317	6.1	.1
Rock Island	2,327	14.6	.6
Springfield			
Sangamon	2,716	17.2	.7
Illinois excluding SMSAs	39,927	19.1	10.2

Source: State of Illinois Department of Public Aid.

Regarding education, Illinois ranked only thirtieth among the states in the number of years spent in school by its adult population, and was slightly below the national average, except for nonwhites.[6] Of the least educated adults in Illinois, of persons with less than an eighth grade education in 1960, three-fourths lived in metropolitan areas and two-thirds in the Chicago and East St. Louis areas.[7] By now, this pattern of geographic distribution will be recognized as similar to that of low income, dependency, and a host of other indicators of deprivation. Virtually all specialized social statistics examined repeat the same areal distributional theme with minor variations.

As for race, the impact on Illinois and its cities of massive rural-urban migrations in the face of segregated housing markets and suburban zoning practices was clearly established a decade ago, and since then, the basic pattern of settlement has not altered. But in the mid-sixties, residential segregation was somewhat intensified by the accelerated mass exodus of middle-class whites to the suburbs. By 1970, the nonwhite population of the state amounted to 1.5 million persons, comprising almost 14% of the total population, as compared with one million persons or 10% of the total population in 1960. However, 86.3% of the state's nonwhite population lived in the Chicago area, 82.7% within Cook County. Another 5.2% lived in the East St. Louis area, while less than 5% were dispersed among the seven other metropolitan areas of the state, and only 3.6% resided in smaller towns or rural places (Table B-5).

In Chicago, the 1970 Census reveals that the population of the six-county area increased over the course of the sixties by 12.2%, but for the first time in its history, the population within the city of Chicago actually declined slightly, by 5.2%. Furthermore, it appears that only an increase of about a quarter of a million black families, coupled with new waves of white immigration, of Appalachians, Hispanic-Americans and foreigners, have sustained the city's population size. Nevertheless, the net white population in the central city declined by 18.6% or by about a half million persons. Thus, the decline of white persons living in Chicago was roughly double the increase in the number of black residents. In absolute numbers, the white population in the city of Chicago is roughly equal to that in 1915.

Black families also moved to the suburbs during the decade but in much smaller numbers than white families and mostly into suburban towns with already established diminutive ghettos. Tallying the net decade changes, only about 3.5% of the total population in the suburban ring of Chicago, in 1970, were black, compared with 2.9% in 1960.[8]

Altogether then, more than one million inhabitants of Chicago, roughly one-third (32.7%), are black, and another 435,000 are Hispanic-American, which when added together with the smaller racial or language minorities living in the city, comprise about half of its total present population. Similar significant population shifts have been observed in the East St. Louis area and in every other large city in Illinois.

None of the above statistics reveals the enormous ethnic, social and cultural heterogeneity of the people presently living in Illinois cities and particularly within the borders of Chicago. Among the immigrants after World War II, the second largest, readily identifiable, minority group is those whose native lan-

Table B-5
Population Distribution in Illinois Metropolitan Areas (SMSA) and Counties by Race, 1970

SMSA and County	Total	Population White	Nonwhite	Nonwhite as Percent of Nonwhite Total in Illinois
Illinois Total	11,113,976	9,600,381	1,513,595	100.0%
Illinois SMSAs	8,903,065	7,443,285	1,459,780	96.4%
Bloomington-Normal	104,389	102,014	2,375	.2%
McLean	104,389	102,014	2,375	.2%
Champaign-Urbana	163,281	150,338	12,943	.9%
Champaign	163,281	150,338	12,943	.9%
Chicago	6,978,947	5,672,570	1,306,377	86.3%
Cook	5,492,369	4,240,896	1,251,473	82.7%
DuPage	491,882	487,871	4,011	.3%
Kane	251,005	241,034	9,971	.7%
Lake	382,638	360,083	22,555	1.5%
McHenry	111,555	111,217	338	–
Will	249,498	231,469	18,029	1.2%
Decatur	125,010	114,899	10,111	.7%
Macon	125,010	114,899	10,111	.7%
East St. Louis	536,110	457,999	78,111	5.2%
Madison	250,934	237,231	13,703	.9%
St. Clair	285,176	220,768	64,408	4.3%
Peoria	341,979	325,984	15,995	1.1%
Peoria	195,318	179,694	15,624	1.0%
Tazewell	118,649	118,391	258	–
Woodford	28,012	27,899	113	–
Rockford	272,063	255,175	16,888	1.1%
Boone	25,440	25,310	130	–
Winnebago	246,623	229,865	16,758	1.1%
Rock Island	219,951	211,182	8,769	.6%
Rock Island	166,734	158,732	8,002	.5%
Henry	53,217	52,450	767	.1%
Springfield	161,335	153,124	8,211	.5%
Sangamon	161,335	153,124	8,211	.5%
Illinois excluding SMSAs	2,210,911	2,157,096	53,815	3.6%

Source: U.S. Bureau of the Census.

guage is Spanish. The immigrants from Mexico, Puerto Rico, Cuba and other Latin American countries, however, are exceedingly diversified in backgrounds, values and skills. As among the blacks and each other racial or ethnic minority aggregated here statistically, great social variation prevails, not only in terms of income, education and occupation, but in life styles as well, in such important matters as child-rearing practices, family stability, sexual-role definition, modes of recreation, authority, prestige and political participation patterns.

To cite an example, many of the political refugees from Cuba arrived with strong vocational and professional skills which facilitated quick assimilation. The levels and conditions of living are severe, however, among Mexican-American migratory farm workers who are beginning to settle in communities in southwest Chicago and in other cities in the northwest corner of Illinois, near food processing plants. Often their children do not attend school, much less have access to medical services or other basic necessities. Their needs and priorities obviously contrast sharply with other Mexican-American families who have lived in Chicago for three generations.

Chicago also contains a Japanese-American population of about 15,000 persons and a Chinese-American population approximating 17,000 persons. The American-Indian population of the city is estimated as near that size, at 17,000, but, in contrast, the latter often live in conditions of extreme hardship and isolation. As for the other racial minorities and ethnic enclaves in the city which retain their identity and language, we have only the dimmest notion of their size. Significant concentrations of Greeks, Yugoslavians, Hungarians, Czechs, Philippinos, Italians, Armenians, Persians, Lithuanians and, of course, Poles (the most numerous), still reside in identifiable neighborhoods in Chicago and still receive a small stream of new immigration. Although an inland city, Chicago is the third largest port of entry in the United States for foreign immigration.

Many of the recent and past immigrants have prospered, and their progeny are now attending the state colleges, the first generation in the family to seek higher education. A student survey at the Circle Campus of the University of Illinois in 1968, for example, revealed that a second language is spoken in one-third of the homes of students presently enrolled, and well over one hundred languages are represented.

Those, however, who arrive with little education and low skills experience great difficulties in making their way, as, for example, the 40,000 white persons who have recently migrated to Chicago from Appalachia. Adding together the estimated sectors of each of the racial, language, ethnic, or otherwise identifiable portion of the groups who came to Chicago in the last decade seeking opportunity and bearing a heritage of deprivation, one finds that a minimum of one-half of the entire population of the city, or about 1.5 million persons, is likely to have encountered difficulties or discrimination on the basis of race, language or cultural style in the job market and in schools.

Appendix C
Organizing a Child-Care
Center, An Example

For the purposes of illuminating the ways in which the interests of a college and a community group might intersect and how a relationship might be structured, a concrete example of a small-scale, service project might be useful. Let us choose a child-care center since they are much needed in poverty areas and since they are relatively simple to organize compared with, let us say, a comprehensive health center. The latter or any number of other projects would serve just as well to illustrate two essential and distinctive organizational features: (1) that the project be autonomous and consumer-oriented; and (2) that teaching or research be integrated with the services offered by the college.

Let us imagine that at a Tenant's Council meeting in a public housing development on the west-side of Chicago, a group of mothers, most of whom are receiving public aid, determine to set up a day-care center so that they may get a job, or take care of the new baby, complete high school, or enter an occupational training program. Having heard that federal funds are available to support such centers and that the Housing Authority will set aside space for one in the project, they seek help in organizing it.

Where do they start? Lots of possibilities are considered and investigated by the tenants. A Model Cities Neighborhood Service Center is about to be established nearby. Many have personal contacts with caseworkers administering public aid and with the local public school. The Department of Labor has several manpower training programs in the area. A settlement house operates an after-school program in their housing project. The Department of Public Health licenses child-care centers, and maybe somebody there would be knowledgeable. Perhaps the local precinct captain could tell them whom to see at City Hall. A West-Side Community Development Corporation has just been organized and, according to a friend who works as a janitor at the Circle Campus of the University of Illinois, some of the people there were very helpful in getting it started. One of their sons is taking a course at Malcolm X College in the evening, and he said that the University of Illinois Medical School helped set up the Valley Health Center over there. One of their daughters is studying to be a nurse's aide at the Amundsen-Mayfair Campus of the City Colleges of Chicago. She heard that they are training neighborhood people to be childcare workers at the Kennedy-King Campus. Northeastern Illinois State College has a neighborhood center in Austin, and Chicago State College has one on Pulaski Boulevard. Both of those schools educate teachers, and if they could find a good teacher first, maybe she would help them get started.

There is no need to elaborate further on the byzantine complexities of programs in poverty neighborhoods as perceived by their residents. The point of the imaginary situation is to suggest that if a college did nothing more than make available to neighborhood groups informed advice and technical assistance about how to proceed, it would be performing an exceedingly useful and singular community service.

Let us carry the story further to the point of actually establishing a center, a model one, in conjunction with a community college which will use it as a base for training students.

Imagine that in investigating the possible ways of proceeding, one of the committee members has had the good fortune to talk with someone at the Circle Campus, where she is told, first, that several faculty members are exceedingly interested in early childhood development and education and would welcome the opportunity to consult with them and, second, that a nearby community college has just expanded its curriculum in early childhood education and is presently seeking supervised, work-study situations for its students. On contacting the community college, the information is confirmed, and in subsequent conversations, it quickly becomes apparent to both groups that their objectives are complimentary and that the center could be structured to serve both their requirements jointly. The Tenant's Council would organize and manage it. The staff would be composed of full-time, licensed nursery school teachers and several child-care or teacher assistants, some of whom would be students-in-training at the college and others, residents of the housing projects who would enroll in the college for part-time study.

To shorten the story, in consultation with the college, the Tenant's Committee threads its way through the labyrinth of governmental grant and licensing procedures. And one fine morning, the model child-care center opens its doors in a vacated apartment in the project to receive 40 of the tenants' children, aged 3 to 5.

Up to this point, only a few features distinguish this child-care center from a dozen others that might be starting up in the neighborhood under other public or private aegis. First, the center is sponsored and operated by a community group who have the responsibility for hiring and firing staff, keeping accounts, ordering supplies, determining admission requirements, program content, and other policy questions. The college makes available to residents whatever assistance and training are necessary to perform leadership and managerial functions effectively.

Second, in the course of organizing the center in collaboration with the college, the tenant's objectives shifted somewhat. They began to focus more and more on the child, his health and nutrition, his behavior in a group, his emotional and intellectual development. Originally conceived primarily as a baby-sitting service, the center was to become an educational venture for both parent and child, and its results were to be evaluated in terms of its effect on each. Health care and meals for the children were included in the initial project design, but other needed, related, educational services and programs for parents were soon added, as in literacy, homemaking, and job training. In consultation with several faculties at the college, educational training facilities were soon grafted into the work of the center, in such related fields as psychological testing, nutrition, business and accounting.

One could stop the story here. Viewing the child-care center as a lever for social change with limited geographic and human perimeters, one could evaluate its effectiveness solely in terms of its direct benefits to the few families served and its secondary effects within the housing development or perhaps the neighborhood. Presumably, the latter might be multiple if the success of the center spawned a group of related projects and programs, embracing other functions and serving other age groups in the family and community. Conceivably, a galaxy of correlated programs might evolve around the center so that the center itself and its satellite projects would be of such excellence as to provide a model for other centers elsewhere, established by other groups and agencies. But to stop here would be still to miss a prime contribution that higher education might make in breaking the cycle of poverty. We have yet to explore higher education's potential role in research, in advancing understanding of human development and of the forces and factors that might influence its course in early childhood.

Let us therefore assume that some of the faculty in a nearby university also became actively involved in the child-care center or in a group of centers, as pilot research projects to test findings in the field and to train students.

Thus, the third feature that might distinguish the child-care center established in consultation with a college or university would be its orientation toward discovery, in this case, toward probing the effects of poverty on a child's early development and toward devising new methods of promoting healthy physical, emotional and intellectual growth.

This is a likely possibility since studies of human behavior confirm the view that the earliest years are particularly formative and that the possibilities of altering personality and behavior are greatest then. For example, in analyzing many longitudinal studies of human development, Benjamin S. Bloom came to the following conclusions.

Of general intelligence (as measured at age seventeen, for both boys and girls), about 50 percent of development takes place between conception and age four, about 30 percent between ages four and eight, and about 20 percent between the ages of eight and seventeen.

As for vocabulary development, reading comprehension, and general school achievement, 33 percent of whatever academic skills children have attained at age eighteen develops between birth and age six, 42 percent between ages six and thirteen, and 25 percent between ages thirteen and eighteen.[1]

In his massive study on equality of educational opportunity, James S. Coleman found that Headstart is often a late start. Black students, tested on entering first grade in northern metropolitan cities, were already about 1.1 standard deviations behind white students tested in the region and the differential in average achievement of minority students widened progressively at progressively higher grade levels.

Whatever may be the combination of nonschool factors—poverty, community attitudes, low educational level of parents—which put minority children at a disadvantage in verbal and nonverbal skills when they enter the first grade, the fact is the schools have not overcome it.[2]

There are many ways that a child-care center or a series of them might be structured to serve both the interests of their organizers in enhancing the life chances of their children and also the interests of particular faculty or students. For example, the latter might investigate the differential effects on child development of more casual baby-sitting arrangements with relatives or neighbors compared with those enrolled in a structured day-care center. To cite another example, pedagogical techniques that have been successfully employed in day-care centers for the disadvantaged in other countries, such as in Israel, the Soviet Union, or Sweden, might be tested in urban slums. Or an anthropologist, studying child-rearing cross-culturally, might examine variations in play and behavior patterns by observing them in a series of day-care centers in different parts of the city, one on the west-side with black children, one perhaps in Lakeview with Spanish-American children, one in Uptown with Appalachian white or American-Indian children, one in Chinatown. Or the day-care center might provide an observation post for psychology students and faculty investigating class- or race-related patterns of play, fantasy, and conceptualization. While such research might seem remote, the insights gained would form the basis of new and more effective teaching or teacher-training programs. Otherwise, they would not be acceptable to the community group sponsoring the day-care center. Research in fields other than child development might also be based at a day-care center, as for example, a cost-effectiveness study of half-day versus full-day programs. Many other possible lines of inquiry with quick potential application are of course conceivable.

It is the application of creative research and new methods, however, that distinguish these kinds of community service projects since the college or university is ultimately accountable to the community group for results. Since cooperation between college and community group is voluntary, when it ceases to be mutually beneficial, the relationship will be dissolved.

While a single, small-scale illustration has been spun out at length to illustrate the proposed approach to service projects in poverty areas, the same principles apply to any number of other projects, equally small in scale and narrowly conceived, as for example, a street academy for high school dropouts or an addiction clinic or to more elaborately designed projects, such as a comprehensive family health center or a community mental health program. In the discussion of the role of the professions in Chapter 9, their application is further explored.

Notes

Notes

Preface

1. Hearings of the Subcommittee on Education, Committee on Labor and Public Welfare, U.S. Senate, First Session on S.600, Part I, March 1965, p. 99.

Chapter 1
The Search for New Ways to Serve

1. *The Assembly on University Goals and Governance: A First Report*, Cambridge: American Academy of Arts and Sciences, 1971.

2. *Report of the President's Commission on Campus Unrest*, reprint edition, New York: Arno Press, 1970.

3. Parker Palmer and Eldon Jacobson, "Urban Experience Labeled 'Middle-Class Voyeurism' " *Chronicle of Higher Education.* 4, #36 (July 6, 1970), p. 7.

Chapter 2
Urban Poverty

1. Eliot L. Richardson, *Chicago Sun-Times*, 1 November 1970; U.S. Bureau of the Census, *Current Population Reports*, Series P-20, No. 190, "School Enrollment: October 1968 and 1967." See also Tables 6-7 and 6-8.

2. Examples include James S. Coleman, *Equality of Educational Opportunity* (U.S. Department of Health, Education and Welfare, 1966); *Racial Isolation in the Public Schools* (U.S. Commission on Civil Rights, 1967); Robert J. Havighurst, *The Public Schools of Chicago* (Chicago: Board of Education, 1964), Chapter 4.

3. U.S. Bureau of the Census, *Current Population Reports*, Consumer Income Series P-60, No. 77. All subsequent statistics cited in this section derive from this source, unless otherwise noted.

4. A detailed account of these issues in a single industrial state, Illinois, is presented in Appendix B.

5. Herman P. Miller, *New York Times*, 12 February 1971.

6. Anthony Downs, *Who are the Urban Poor*, rev. ed. (New York: Committee for Economic Development, Supplementary Paper No. 26, 1970).

7. *Poverty Amid Plenty: The American Paradox*, Report of the President's Commission on Income Maintenance Programs (Washington, D.C., 1969).

8. U.S. Bureau of the Census, *Current Population Reports*, Consumer Income Series P-60, No. 77.

9. *Manpower Report of the President*, U.S. Department of Labor, Washington, D.C.: March 1970.

10. *Poverty Amid Plenty: The American Paradox*.

11. *New York Times*, 4 February 1971.

12. Survey conducted by Louis Harris and Associates for the National Reading Council, *New York Times*, 12 September 1970.

13. Study by David Harman, *New York Times*, 19 May 1970.

14. The above estimates of population changes were released by the Bureau of the Census, and reported in the *New York Times*, 11 February 1971. Although preliminary, proportionate relationships are unlikely to differ when the final count figures from the 1970 Census are released.

15. Ibid.

16. Ibid.

17. Ibid., 4 March 1971.

18. Ibid.

19. Ibid.

20. *Chicago Sun-Times*, 15 October 1970. For a recent study of school expenditures in Michigan which found that intradistrict inequalities were of a greater magnitude than interdistrict inequalities, see Thomas, J. Alan, *School Finance and Educational Opportunity in Michigan* (Lansing: Michigan Department of Education, 1968); for a general account, see also Harry M. Levin, "Financing Education for the Urban Disadvantaged," in *Resources for Urban Schools: Better Use and Balance*, Committee for Economic Development (Lexington, Massachusetts: Heath-Lexington Books, 1971).

21. For further discussion, see Alice L. Ebel, "Local Government Outside Cook County," in *Con-Con*, edited by S.K. Gore, and V. Ranney, (Urbana: University of Illinois Press, 1970).

22. Jack Meltzer, and Joyce Whitley, "Social and Physical Planning In the Urban Slum," in *Goals for Urban America*, edited by B.J.L. Berry, and Jack Meltzer, (Englewood Cliffs, N.J.: Prentice-Hall, Inc., 1967).

23. For a discussion of a small-area social statistics, see Doris B. Holleb, *Social and Economic Information for Urban Planning* (Chicago: Center for Urban Studies, University of Chicago, 1969).

Chapter 3
Poverty Policies

1. Downs, *Who Are Urban Poor?*

2. *Manpower Report of the President*, U.S. Department of Labor (Washington, D.C.: 1971).

3. Ibid.

4. Jane Altes, *East St. Louis: End of A Decade* (Edwardsville: Southern Illinois University, 1970).

5. "BLS Reports on Economic Problems for West Side Neighborhoods of Chicago." Mimeo. Bureau of Labor Statistics, U.S. Department of Labor. (1969).

6. Illinois State Employment Service et al., *New Dimensions in Manpower* (Illinois, 1968).

7. *Manpower Report of the President*, U.S. Department of Labor (January 1969).

8. *Occupational Outlook Handbook*, U.S. Department of Labor, Bulletin No. 1650 (1970).

Chapter 4
Roles and Routes for Higher Education

1. *Extension and Public Service in the University of Illinois: Phase I Report (November 1967).*

Chapter 5
Widening Opportunities

1. See for example the following: W.L. Hansen, and B.A. Weisbrod, *Benefits Costs and Finance of Public Higher Education* (Chicago: Markham Publishing Company, 1969); Joseph A. Pechman, "The Distributional Effects of Public Higher Education in California," *Journal of Human Resources*, 2, no. 3; "Higher Education, Equity and Efficiency," C.O.B.R.E. Mimeo. (University of Chicago, 1971); Edw. F. Denison, "An Aspect of Unequal Opportunity" *Journal of Political Economy* (Sept./Oct. 1970).

2. Alice M. Rivlin, and June O'Neil, "Growth and Change in Higher Education," *The Corporation and the Campus*, Proceedings of The Academy of Political Science 30, no. 1 (1970).

3. Unless otherwise indicated, statistics cited in this section are derived from U.S. Bureau of the Census, from recent Current Population Reports.

4. *New York Times*, 4 February 1971.

5. "College Educated Workers, 1968-80," Bulletin #1676, Bureau of Labor Statistics, U.S. Department of Labor (1970).

6. *The Open-Door College*, Carnegie Commission on Higher Education (New Jersey: McGraw-Hill, June 1970).

7. James W. Trent, and Leland L. Medsker, *Beyond High School* (San Francisco: Jossey-Bass, 1968).

8. Unless otherwise indicated, all basic data about Illinois enrollments, past, present and projected, came from the two sources listed below. In some cases, additional arithmetic computations were undertaken with these basic statistics. G.J. Froelich, and R.D. Carey, *Higher Educational Enrollment in Illinois,*

1960-2000, University Bureau of Institutional Research (Urbana: University of Illinois, 1969). G.J. Froelich, and A.R. Luandowski, *Enrollments in Institutions of Higher Learning in Illinois* (Urbana: University Bureau of Institutional Research, University of Illinois, 1969).

9. Allan M. Cartter, "Scientific Manpower for 1970-1985," *Science* 172 (April 9, 1971); *New Students and New Places: Policies for the Future Growth and Development of Higher Education*, The Carnegie Commission on Higher Education, New Jersey (McGraw-Hill, 1971).

10. "Educational Attainment, March 1970," U.S. Bureau of the *Census Current Population Reports*, Series P-20, No. 207.

11. All statistics on female employment reported here come from *Handbook on Women Workers*, Women's Bureau Bulletin 294, U.S. Department of Labor (1969).

12. Joseph Froomkin, *Aspiration, Enrollments and Resources*, U.S. Department of Health, Education and Welfare (1970).

13. A point emphasized in discussions with Dr. Robert J. Havighurst.

14. Harold L. Hodgkinson, *Institutions in Transition: A Study of Change in Higher Education* (Berkeley: Carnegie Commission for Higher Education, 1970).

15. Ibid.

16. See *New Students and New Places; Less Time, More Options: Education Beyond the High School*, The Carnegie Commission on Higher Education (New Jersey: McGraw-Hill, 1971); *Report on Higher Education*, U.S. Department of Health, Education and Welfare (March 1971).

Chapter 6
Sources of Inequality

1. "Characteristics of American Youth: 1970," Current Population Reports, P-23, No. 34, U.S. Bureau of the Census (February 1, 1971).

2. U.S. Bureau of the Census, 1970.

3. Alan Sorkin, "Poverty and Dropouts, the Case of the American Indian," in *Growth and Change* 1, no. 3 (University of Kentucky, 1970).

4. James S. Coleman, *Equality of Educational Opportunity*, U.S. Department of Health, Education and Welfare (1966).

5. Estimate of The College Entrance Examination Board, Princeton, N.J.

6. A special estimate prepared for and cited in *Priorities in Higher Education: The Report of the President's Task Force on Higher Education* (August 1970).

7. Fred E. Crossland, *Minority Access to College: A Ford Foundation Report* (New York: Schocken Books, 1971).

8. Ibid.

9. A more detailed analysis of the *Project Talent* data is to be found in

J.K. Folger, H.S. Astin, and A.E. Bayer, *Human Resources and Higher Education* (New York: Russell Sage Foundation, 1970), Chapter 10.

10. Richard Pearson, *The Opening Door, A Review of New York State's Program of Financial Aid for College Students* (N.Y.: College Entrance Examination Board, 1967).

11. Lee W. Hansen, and Burton A. Weisbrod, *Benefits, Costs, and Finance of Public Higher Education* (Chicago: Markham, 1969).

12. For details, see Meyer Weinberg, "The Economic-Fiscal Setting of Educational Opportunity: The City Colleges of Chicago in the 1970s." Mimeo. (City College of Chicago, 1970).

13. Precise data are not available in useful form. The figures cited here are informed and informal estimates of knowledgeable people working in the public schools, such as high school principals.

Chapter 7
Reducing the Obstacles

1. National Association of State Universities and Land Grant Colleges.

2. Warren W. Willingham, *Free Access to Higher Education* (New York: College Entrance Examination Board, 1970).

3. See, for example, The Newman Task Force *Report on Higher Education*; The American Assembly on Goals and Governance: A First Report; *Less Time, More Options*, The Carnegie Commission on Higher Education; A.J. Peters, *British Further Education* (Oxford: Pergamon Press, 1967); *Higher Education and National Affairs* (February 9, 1971); *The Chronicle of Higher Education* (March 22, 1971).

Chapter 8
Extending Services to the Poor

1. Harold A. Richman, "Financial Assistance and Social Services," in *Delivery Systems for Model Cities*, edited by E.N. Williams (University of Chicago: Center for Policy Study and Center for Urban Studies, 1969).

2. Jack Meltzer, and William Swenson, "New Principles and Mechanisms in the Model Cities Plan of the Woodlawn Organization," in *Delivery Systems for Model Cities*.

3. Jack Meltzer, and Leon D. Finney, "Remarks," in *Woodlawn's Model Cities Plan: A Demonstration of Citizen Responsibility* (Northbrook, Ill.: Whitehall Co., 1970).

Chapter 9
The Professions and Systemic Reform

1. *New York Times*, 6 June 1971.
2. Alan Gartner, and Harriet Johnson, *An Examination of College Programs for Para Professionals* (New York University: New Careers Development Center, October 1971).
3. J.K. Folger, H.S. Astin, and A.E. Bayer, *Human Resources and Higher Education* (New York: Russell Sage Foundation, 1970) and Allan M. Cartter, "Scientific Manpower for 1970-1985," *Science* 172 (April 9, 1971).
4. Many recent studies have emphasized the need to revamp the health care system including *Report of the National Advisory Commission on Health Manpower*, Vol. 1; U.S. Department of Health, Education and Welfare (1967).
5. *Chicago Sun-Times*, 29 September 1970.
6. *New York Times*, 31 May 1971.
7. Ibid., 30 May 1971.
8. *Chicago Sun-Times*, 8 September 1970.
9. Welfare Council of Metropolitan Chicago, *Social Welfare Manpower Needs in the Chicago Area* (Chicago, 1968).
10. Myrna B. Kassel, ed., *Manpower for Human Services*, 1, no. 1 (Illinois Department of Labor, Bureau of Employment Security, 1970).
11. Ibid.
12. *New York Times*, 12 July 1971.
13. Ibid., 28 August 1970.
14. For a discussion by its Director of some of the issues raised by the experience, see Jack H. Geiger, M.D., "Hidden Professional Roles: The Physician as Reactionary, Reformer, Revolutionary," *Social Policy* 1, no. 6 (March/April 1971).
15. See *Chicago Tribune*, 25 March 1971.

Chapter 10
The Campus and Climate of Cooperation

1. *The President's Report, 1969-70* (Cambridge, Massachusetts: Harvard University, 1970).
2. Ibid.
3. *New York Times*, 4 February 1970.

Chapter 11
Generating a Statewide and Metropolitan Response

1. *Priorities in Higher Education*. Report of the President's Task Force on Higher Education (August 1970). See especially pp. 14-17.

171

2. *The Behavioral and Social Sciences: Outlook and Needs*, A report by The Behavioral and Social Sciences Survey Committee under the auspices of The Committee on Science and Public Policy, National Academy of Sciences, The Committee of Problems and Policy, Social Science Research Council (New Jersey: Prentice-Hall, 1969).

3. Ibid.

4. Paul F. Lazarsfeld, and Samuel D. Sieber, *Reforming the University: The Role of the Research Center* (New York: Columbia University, Bureau of Applied Research, 1971).

5. *The Behavioral and Social Sciences: Outlook and Needs*.

6. The findings of this study, conducted by Karl W. Deutsch, John R. Platt, and Dieter Senghaas under the auspices of the Mental Health Research Institute of the University of Michigan, were reported in the *New York Times*, 16 March 1971 in advance of publication.

7. See discussion of Illinois enrollments by race in Chapter 6, pp. 67-74.

Appendix B
Urbanization, Poverty and Race in Illinois

1. Chicago Association of Commerce and Industry.

2. U.S. Census of Population, 1960.

3. Estimates prepared by Pierre DeVise for Hospital Planning Council, Chicago Regional Hospital Study, 1968.

4. Ibid.

5. Jane Altes, *East St. Louis: End of A Decade* (Edwardsville: Southern Illinois University, 1970).

6. *Ranking of the States*, 1968, National Education Association Report No. RR-1968-R1, 1968.

7. U.S. Census of Population, 1960.

8. Ibid., 1970.

Appendix C
Organizing a Child-Care Center, An Example

1. Muriel Beadle, *A Child's Mind* (Garden City, New York: Doubleday and Company, 1970).

2. James S. Coleman, *Equality of Educational Opportunity*, U.S. Department of Health, Education and Welfare (1966).

Index

Afro-American programs 98

Agricultural extension, 50–51, 98, 125

Allied-Health Institute, City College of Chicago, 37

Amundsen-Mayfair campus, City College of Chicago, 69

Association of American Law Schools, 111

Attrition, 75, 82–84

Berry, Brian J. L., *xvi*

Barzun, Jacques, 4

Birenbaum, William, 4

Blacks: dropout rates among, 66; in central cities, 33; increase of enrollment in colleges and universities of, 56, 57*t*, 63, 66–67; migration of, 21; poverty among, 13–14; unemployment among, 34

Bloom, Benjamin S., 161

Boston University, 126

Boyd, R. Samuel, *xvi*

Brail, Richard, *xvi*

Brewster, Kingman, Jr., 77

Bureau of the Census, 14, 17, 21, 65, 66

Career ladders, 107–108, 110, 114

Carnegie Commission on Higher Education, 61, 167, 168, 169

Census, 1970, 17, 65, 150, 157

Center for Urban Studies, University of Chicago, *xiv, xv, xvi*

Central YMCA College, 60

Chicago State College, 37, 69, 75, 102; enrollment in by race, 73*t*

Child-Care centers, 104, 108, 159–162

Child Health Associates, 110

Circle Campus of the University of Illinois, 16, 28–29, 36–37, 67, 81, 92, 102, 137–138, 141, 143

City Colleges of Chicago, 37, 68, 81, 82, 90; enrollment in by race, 70–71*t*

City University of New York, 58, 82, 87, 115, 144

Clark, Kenneth B., 112

Coleman, James S., 161–162

Colleges: enrollment by family income, 78*t*; enrollment by race, 56*t*; future enrollments, 60–63; governance, 131, 142–144; increased enrollment, 55–63; segregation, 23–24, 67, 74, 139–141

Columbia University, 126, 136

Columbia University Law School, 111

Community Colleges, articulation of curricula, 91, 107–108; defacto segregation

in, 24, 69, 70*t*–73*t*; financing of, 90, 134, 140; governance, 131, 142–144; growth, 58*t*–59; mission, 49, 59, 68, 90, 124–125, 132–134; neighborhood role, 92, 124–125; paraprofessional education, 107; vocational education, 132–133

Community development projects, 115–116, 127–128

Community participation, 98, 102–104, 119, 124, 126

Community service, 1–7, 43, 46–48, 97–104, 115–119, 127–128

Counseling, 87–88

Dahlke, Jerry, *xvi*

Department of Labor, 123

Department of Local Government Affairs, Illinois, 114

Department of Mental Health, Illinois, 114

Diversity among colleges, 63–64, 93–94, 144

Division of Vocational and Technical Education, Illinois, 114

Duke University, 110

East St. Louis: community college in, 69, 90; 1969 survey of, 34–35

Education Commission of the States, 117–118

Education, adult, 86, 91–93; funding for, 129–132, 141

Education, attainment of by race, 57*t*

Education, higher: expansion of, 55–59; future demand for, 60–63; inequalities in access to, 45–48, 65–84; reducing inequalities, 85–94; stratification in, 49–50, 139

Education, professional, 44, 103, 105, 107, 108–113, 115–118

Employment Act of 1946, 32

Employment: racial discrimination in, 33–34; status by race, sex, and age, 35*t*; of women, 62–63; trends, 39–40

Financial barriers to higher education, 75–80; eliminating, 85–88, 129–130, 132, 134

Financial constraints on colleges, 45, 51, 129–131, 139

Fleishman, Joel L., *xvi*

Goldberg, Lawrence, *xvi*

Goodman, Paul, 4

173

About the Author

Doris B. Holleb is an economist and urban planner. Research Associate at the Center for Urban Studies of the University of Chicago since 1966, Mrs. Holleb has written and lectured extensively about urban problems, social policies and urban information systems, including recent articles on social indicators, a mid-decade census, metropolitan development and residential segregation. A prior book, *Social and Economic Information for Urban Planning*, exemplifies the application of the social sciences to the resolution of practical problems, as does this book. A Phi Beta Kappa graduate of Hunter College with an M.A. in Economics from Harvard, her knowledge of urban affairs has been deepened in her work with governmental agencies on current policy questions. She has served as consultant to a number of federal agencies, including the Departments of Housing and Urban Development, Health, Education and Welfare, and the Federal Reserve Board and to such local agencies as the Chicago Department of Development and Planning and the Illinois Board of Higher Education. She also serves on the newly created Advisory Council of the Illinois Superintendent of Public Instruction and is a former member of the Citizens Advisory Committee of the Illinois Board of Higher Education.